VITAMINS AND MINERALS

A Comprehensive Guide to
Understanding Your Daily Diet and Nutrition

Eleanor Stillwell

ISLAND BOOKS

This edition published in 2002 by
S.WEBB & SON (Distributors) LTD,
Telford Place, Penraeth Road, Menai Bridge,
Isle of Anglesey, LL59 5RW

Produced in 2002 by PRC Publishing Ltd.
64 Brewery Road, London, N7 9NT
A member of **Chrysalis** Books plc

ISBN 1 85605 746 1

Printed and bound in Taiwan

Contents

At every stage of life we have different
nutritional requirements.

INTRODUCTION

We are all becoming more health conscious nowadays and the journey to better health and a proper balanced diet is seemingly helped along the way by the variety of useful advice that fills up shelves at the bookstore. Much of this advice is written by senior health professionals who really believe that—under the right circumstances—their way is best. But it is not so easy to work out which practitioner gives the best advice, and just because the latest fad diet has worked for several celebrities doesn't always means it is going to work for you. There is also a lot of advice given out by the government, but what have you understood about the information that has been bandied about in the press with respect to diet and health issues?

The main message to understand is that, along with trying to sort out a manageable work-life balance, we also have to organize our personal lifestyle-diet balance. Many of us fail to realize how our eating habits can contribute to a less healthy body, and how, as we get older, our energy needs change. Men and women also have different nutritional requirements, as do athletes in training when compared to the not quite so active gym visitor.

A healthy diet is easy to achieve and can be enjoyable too! It is important that everyone, young or old, maintains a healthy diet because frequently it can help prevent a variety of nasty diseases— heart disease, tooth decay, obesity, osteoporosis—while also actively protecting us against other serious illnesses. We know that heart disease, diabetes, high blood pressure, and other major ailments, including several cancers, can in part be directly linked to poor nutrition. Many

people believe that a change in diet can have a greater impact on public health than drugs. Why should this be the case?

In the last 100 years the variety of food available and the processing of food has brought about a revolution in our eating habits and not all of them good. We now eat more refined carbohydrate (starches and sugars) than ever before, more ready-prepared meals, and more junk food. If we compare our current diet with a typical diet from the early 20th century we see

Left and above: Over the past 50 years, particularly for those living in the northern hemisphere, the produce reaching our markets has become more exciting and exotic.

that we eat a much higher percentage of saturated fat, more refined and processed food, and not enough fruit and vegetables. It should also be noted that at the same time the incidence of heart disease has risen exponentially and we lead much less active lifestyles than our grandparents' generation did. Official surveys by US and EC Departments of Health show that most people obtain more than enough calories, protein, and fat from a modern diet, but that it is lacking in many of the essential nutrients such as vitamins, essential minerals, trace minerals, antioxidants, and essential fatty acids. The United States Congress recently got to the crux of the matter: "Never have so many people been so well-fed and yet so badly nourished." On the plus side however, food shops and supermarkets are bursting with both local and exotic produce. The variety has greatly expanded when compared with our great grandparents' time: today we can eat food from virtually every corner of the world.

This book will try to guide you toward adopting a more nutritiously delicious and balanced diet, by which you can achieve a healthier lifestyle.

WHAT IS A BALANCED DIET?

The message from many professionals is that a balanced diet involves less fat, more fruit, and more fiber. But by following this mantra do we always get it right? Recently some scientific studies have shown that we should in fact be eating the right sorts of foods, and that reducing our intake of sugary carbohydrates, and increasing our intake of protein-

A favorite meal of many people, but too much junk food really isn't good for you.

rich foods may actually be a better way to eat. We have come to have a great reliance on carbohydrates, particularly sugars, at the expense of more nutritious—and highly tasty—foods. There is a good case for looking more closely at and returning to our ancestor's diets; the incidences of major illnesses were less, in fact some were unheard of.

The function of food is to provide the body with the necessary nutrients, in as pleasant a form as possible, that can be processed for particular uses, primarily energy supply. For peak performance, we should get a good balance of the variety of nutrients from the four major food groups. These are:

- **the milk group:** milk, cheese, yogurt.
- **the meat group:** which includes nuts, beans, eggs, poultry, seafood.
- **the fruit and vegetable group:** all fruit and vegetables.
- **the bread and cereal group:** whole or enriched grains including bread, pasta, rice, noodles etc.

The best way to achieve a balanced diet is to eat a variety of foods from all the different food groups, eat at least one balanced meal a day, and limit, preferably avoid, unhealthy snacks. Due to the fantastic antioxidant effects and the abundance of vitamins and minerals in fruit and vegetables, we are also encouraged to ensure that we eat five to seven portions of fruit and vegetables a day. Our carbohydrates should be largely unrefined and with a low glycaemic index—that is less white bread, more whole grain, reduced sugar, and more pulses. We should also eat more seafood, a perhaps surprising source of many essential nutrients. By doing this, not only should you fulfill your energy requirements but also easily address your body's basic vitamin and mineral requirements, and then some.

MEDITERRANEAN DIET

You will have heard about the wonder of the Mediterranean diet which is seemingly high in fat, with a splash of alcohol. Scientists have studied it carefully because the people of the Mediterranean coastline and associated countries who thrive on this particular way of eating also have reduced incidences of heart disease and other ailments usually associated with industrialization. One reason is that they eat a high proportion of fresh fruit and vegetables, low glycaemic index foods, a range of meat, and a lot of fish. The way they cook is also important, as is the use of olive oil. Overall the diet is lower in saturated fat and higher in micronutrients (that is vitamins, minerals, etc.), and it can actively lower blood pressure and reduce the risk of coronary heart disease. The Mediterranean lifestyle may also be a crucial factor: meals are savored not rushed, which is always better for digestion.

The components of a typical Mediterranean meal—healthy, tasty, and full of protective antioxidants.

EXERCISE

It should not be forgotten that part of a healthy lifestyle includes a portion of exercise too. Any exercise can go a long way to help, but three to four sessions a week, each about 30 minutes long will bring about noticeable beneficial improvements to your health. The changes necessary to incorporate exercise may not be as major as you think; you don't have to visit a sports center, just start walking or cycling to places rather than talking the car. The main thing about the form of exercise you choose is that you should be able to enjoy and maintain it, but be prepared to try a variety of things to decide what works for you.

Exercise is easy when you are young, making the time to fit it into a busy life can be beneficial.

VITAMINS AND MINERALS

A healthy diet includes five to seven portions of fruit and vegetables a day.

Where do vitamins and minerals fit into this picture? We are not just talking about popping a multivitamin or several different supplements, as many people do as a form of health insurance. It is a fact that most people don't manage to eat the recommended number of portions of fruit and vegetables and as a result are probably not reaping the benefits, which over a lifetime can prove to be many. The aim of the following chapters is to show you where you can find the best sources of each vitamin and mineral, and also how they fit into the wider picture of a healthy lifestyle, at no matter what your stage of life.

Vitamins are organic substances and most are cofactors for metabolic enzymes which are crucial for complete and successful digestion. They help keep our bodies in delicately balanced equilibrium. If the equilibrium is upset, symptoms usually show in the form of minor ailments, or when severe as deficiency disease. Insufficient uptake of a particular vitamin can lead to a deficiency, for instance a lack of vitamin D can lead to rickets. Vitamins are classified as either fat-soluble or water-soluble. Fat-soluble ones, particularly A and D, are stored in the liver and can be toxic (poisonous) in excess. The water-soluble vitamins (C and B group), if not used within the body will just be excreted, and it therefore follows that we need a fairly continuous supply. While many vitamins and minerals have vital functions at a cellular level, only minute quantities are required, and our cells don't ever stop working. Also important is the fact that, with a few exceptions, we are not able to manufacture these essentials components of our diet. You can't just take a handful of supplements to make things better; vitamins supplements are not substitutes for real food, and they cannot be assimilated without food. They have no calorific value, but many practitioners believe they can have an overall beneficial effect on your health.

An analogy often quoted is that of the body as a car, where the vitamins are the spark plugs. They regulate our metabolism through a network of enzyme systems, some of which require specific minerals to function correctly as well. You can gain optimum performance from this "car" by using the correct "fuel," but occasionally the "spark plugs" need cleaning, adjusting, or replacing. So it is that there are times in your life when extra vitamins or minerals will be required, and if you are unable to acquire them as food, then a nutrient supplement is better than nothing, and is likely to have a positive effect.

A well-balanced diet should include the following vitamins and minerals which cannot be stored in the body, although specific requirements vary from person to person: vitamins A, B group, C, D, and

E, along with the minerals, iron, calcium, phosphorus, magnesium, sodium, potassium, zinc, and trace elements copper, iodine, fluorine, selenium, and chromium. In addition, much care should be taken not to take amounts over the recommended daily allowance, as there are various vitamins and minerals that can be stored in the body and excess can prove toxic.

Women have very specific nutritional needs throughout life and should carefully consider their vitamin and mineral intake for optimum health.

It is a fact that many people take a range of vitamin supplements to combat the effects of a convenience food diet and stress, to protect against disease, or to slow down the aging process. A general multivitamin could help to boost your body's defenses against minor infections, but there are also groups of people who have extra requirements and who may benefit from supplements. These include:

- Those with poor diets (such as the elderly) or choosy eaters (such as faddy children).
- Peoples on restricted diets: celiac, vegan, diabetic.
- People convalescing or with poor immune systems.
- Those with digestive disorders, food intolerances.
- Women, either when menstruating, pregnant, or breast feeding.
- Smokers and drinkers.
- Athletes and very active people.

16

Almonds, like most nuts, are full of essential minerals and
vitamins, high in protein and unsaturated fat.

As already mentioned, in addition to vitamins we need a supply of essential minerals. Many of the minerals we require are inorganic metals, and 20 have been classified as essential to our diets. These can be divided into major minerals and trace elements. They are used as components of bones and teeth; as salts to regulate body fluids; and as constituents of enzymes and hormones. They are present in most kinds of food but the amounts vary and can be particularly dependent upon the type of soil where food crops are grown. They exist as mineral salts in nature and it is these compounds that are used in supplements. Minerals are best supplied as organic salts, that is those containing carbon atoms, as they are absorbed more readily by the body.

With all these factors in mind, this book will examine more closely the role of vitamins and minerals to our lives. Where possible it will also look at suggested doses of vitamin and mineral supplements correlating to particular circumstances; when they should be taken, how effective they are, and any downsides to taking nutritional supplements. In addition, in order to provide a rounded approach, this book will also look closely at the other components of a healthy diet including: proteins and amino acids; fats, fatty acids, and lipotropics; carbohydrates and the implications of recently published works on the glycaemic index. The last chapter will be a summary of the information; it looks at requirements for different stages of life, from babies to the elderly, indicating what is suitable for busy people of all ages. The aim is to help you decipher the many factors involved in healthy living, including the impact of lifestyle, sport, family life, work, and illness on both your body and your nutritional status.

Right: Children who are active and growing need the right nutritional support to help them be healthy adults.

1. VITAMINS

Nutritionists have devised a couple of terms to describe and group the various nutrients we get from our food. Carbohydrates, protein, and fats are components of a healthy diet that we require in large quantities and are termed **macronutrients**. These are discussed in more detail in later chapters. Vitamins and minerals are required in minute amounts and are termed **micronutrients**. The next two sections look at these micronutrients, what they are, where they can be found, and what they do for us.

What are vitamins?

Vitamins are organic compounds. We are unable to synthesize most of them, so we require a regular supply which we get through our daily food intake. A balanced diet contains an adequate amount of all micronutrients. The vitamins we can synthesize include vitamin D, which is synthesized in the body to a limited degree (the action of sunlight on the skin converts cholesterol to vitamin D), and vitamins B12 and K, which are synthesized by bacterial flora in the intestinal tract.

Vitamins are classified as either water- or fat-soluble. The B complex and vitamin C are water-soluble; vitamins A, D, E, and K are fat-soluble. The body can store only a limited amount of water-soluble vitamins and they are rapidly excreted in the urine if ingested in greater quantities than the body requires. B12 is exceptional to this as it is stored in the liver, and the stores can last for years. Deficiency diseases

Left: Food that's good for you frequently looks tasty.
This lot will supply a whole range of vital vitamins and minerals.

are more likely to occur with water-soluble vita-mins. Food preparation can easily damage them: prolonged cooking, storage, and processing all take their toll, so it is better to use fresh, lightly cooked foods. Frozen fruit and vegetables also tend to retain higher levels of vitamins than their stored counterparts.

Fat-soluble vitamins are absorbed with fats in the intestine into the bloodstream and then stored in fatty tissue, mainly the liver. Reserves of these vitamins in the body can last a very long time, sometimes years, and a daily intake is not essential. Excessive intake of fat-soluble vitamins may in fact be harmful, especially of vitamin D.

Best eaten fresh and in season, asparagus is a great all round vitamin provider and natural diuretic.

What do vitamins do?

We still do not have the complete picture of the role of vitamins with-in the body. Most vitamins have several important actions on one or more body systems, and many are cofactors for enzymes that are important to metabolic function.

We are more likely to be affected by insufficient uptake of vitamins than excess intake: most are not harmful in excess quantities (see separate entries below). Insufficient quantities of particular vitamins can cause deficiency diseases to a greater or lesser degree. A well-known example is lack of vitamin C causing scurvy.

Right: All citrus fruits are packed with vitamin C.

Scurvy was the first deficiency disease to be recognized as it was the first to be easily cured with food: by about 1720 it was known that fresh vegetables or fruit could reverse the symptoms of the disease. In 1757 a physician in the British navy, James Lind, showed that consumption of citrus fruit such as oranges and lemons could prevent the disease. Captain James Cook adopted the principles of this discovery and as a result had scurvy-free voyages. In 1804 the British navy made it compulsory for rations of lemons or limes to be issued which resulted in the sailors being nicknamed "limeys."

A primary function of many vitamins is an involvement in metabolic enzyme reactions. If a combination of essential factors including vitamins and minerals are not present, then metabolic reactions proceed too slowly to be effective. This further leads to malabsorption disorders. These disorders are a main factor in deficiency diseases; they occur when dietary nutrients are not absorbed in the small intestine and can be due to a combination of factors.

When do we need supplements?

A physician may recommend or prescribe dietary supplements of vitamins in specific circumstances:

• Where an unusual diet is obviously deficient in vitamins causing insufficient intake. In developed countries this most often occurs in people on a poor diet, caused by low income, lack of interest in

Even during regular exercise we place demands on our bodies to perform; without a healthy diet we might not enjoy it so much.

food, or an alcohol or drug dependence. A vegan diet may sometimes be lacking the full complement of micronutrients. People being feed intravenously or via a tube are more likely to need supplements.

• Conditions or diseases resulting in poor intestinal absorption (caused by disease or by therapeutic drugs).

• In relatively healthy individuals there are occasions—during times of growth, hard physical work, pregnancy, lactation, and menstruation—when there are greater requirements by various body tissues for an increased supply of essential nutrients.

• Disorders such as hyperthyroidism, infectious diseases accompanied by fever, and tissue-wasting diseases, also cause increased requirements.

Some vitamins are used to treat disorders that are not specifically a deficiency. For instance vitamin D is used in the treatment of osteoporosis.

Vitamins are often regarded as unseen components of a healthy diet. We are discovering more about them all the time. Recommended daily allowances (RDAs) have been calculated for all ages. In the UK reference nutrient intakes or RNIs are also used, and they indicate the recommended daily amount for 97 percent of all adults. The RDAs for all micronutrients are different for children, and men and women at particular times of life, such as through puberty, and when a woman is pregnant or breast feeding.

Both the EC and USA RDA allowances were originally intended as a guide for people involved in the food industry particularly with regard to food labeling, planning supplies, and the analysis of food consumption levels. It should be noted though, that RDA figures are only estimates based on current knowledge of the needs of most people. Personal daily requirements will actually depend on many factors individual to each person such as genetics, environmental influences, and presence or absence of disease.

Garlic is a great component of any diet, able to act in many ways to confer better health. If you don't like the taste, garlic pills would be a good substitute.

How are they measured?

As described on page 231 there are various units used in the measurements of vitamins. Vitamins A, D, E, and K are frequently measured in international units (IU). Most others are measured in milligrams (mg) and micrograms (µg). Vitamin A is the exception. It recently been suggested by the World Health Organization and the Food and Agriculture Organization (WHO/FAO) that a more accurate measure of vitamin A is to describe it in terms of the amount of retinol actually absorbed and converted. This measurement is termed retinol equivalents (RE) and values work out five times less than international units.

Vitamin supplements usually contain somewhere in the range of one-half to one-and-a-half times the RDA values. The exceptions are vitamin D, which should not exceed 400IU, and vitamin A, which should not exceed 1,000RE. Multivitamin formulations are designed to help prevent illness and to augment the diet in times of unusual stress. Single supplements usually have higher strengths and should be taken with caution and under the guidance of a doctor.

Do you know how digestion works?

Many vitamin deficiencies are the result of malabsorption disorders in the intestines. But the functions of many enzymes are also closely involved in the digestive process as well. Here is probably the best place to run through how the digestive process works, so that you can better understand both the means of action of vitamins and how deficiencies can arise.

At stages during the digestive process various enzymes are secreted by the body. These are biological catalysts that ensure that the breakdown of food happens and at the optimum rate (for more information see chapter four). Digestion begins with the chewing of food in the mouth; saliva contains enzymes that begin to break down starches

*Broad beans and apples are a good source of soluble fiber
which will help the digestion process work more smoothly.*

Eating bio yogurt is great way to replenish intestinal bacteria, particularly after a stomach upset. Normal yogurt is a rich source of calcium and protein, but watch out for large amounts of sugar in fruit yogurts.

while the food travels down the esophagus by a mechanism called peristalsis (waves of muscle contraction). In the stomach gastric juices are secreted that contain hydrochloric acid (required for the action of pepsin), pepsin (main digester of meat and other proteins), renin (curdles milk), and a factor that enables B12 to be absorbed. Practically the only substances absorbed directly through the stomach wall is water and alcohol. Liquids leave the stomach quite rapidly but more solid substances will remain three to five hours before a sphincter relaxes and allows it to move into the small intestine.

The small intestine (which has identifiable sections known as the duodenum, jejunum, and ileum) is where the absorption of most nutrients takes place. Bile, pancreatic juice, and intestinal wall secretions create an alkaline environment necessary for the main digestive processes. Produced in the liver, bile is stored in the gall bladder, and while not all its contents are involved in digestion it does contain substances that emulsify fats. The pancreas releases insulin directly into the blood stream, which has an effect on blood-sugar levels and a collection of enzymes (pancreatic juice): lipases (which break down fats), proteases (which breakdown protein), and amylases which continue to split starches. The intestinal walls also secrete additional digestive enzymes which work on carbohydrates and polypeptides. Along with the products of digestion of macronutrients, some water, inorganic salts, and vitamins are absorbed in the small intestine.

The partially liquid contents are moved along the intestinal tract by peristaltic movements and eventually reach the large intestine, or colon. As the material travels through the colon—a process that can take around 15 hours—water is absorbed and very little else. A large number of intestinal bacteria reside in the colon, and these mix with the indigestible fiber along with other waste products. This forms the feces which are excreted.

What's in a name?

When the first vitamins were discovered, the finer points of their chemical structures were not completely deciphered and they were designated letters from the alphabet in lieu of proper nomenclature. This naming system is still used, but you may also see their chemical names or compounds in labels as well. The following vitamins have been written about: some are better known than others.

A (retinol); B complex: B1 (thiamine), B2 (riboflavin), B3 (niacin), B5 (pantothenic acid), B6 (pyridoxine), B10, B11 (growth factors), B12 (cyanocobalamine), B13 (orotic acid), B15 (pangamic acid), B17 (amygdalin), choline, inositol; C (ascorbic acid); D (calciferol); E (tocopherols); F (fatty acids); G (riboflavin); H (biotin); K (menadine); L (needed for lactation); M (folic acid); P (bioflavinoids); T (growth promotion factors); U (extracted from cabbage juice).

Eggs are a good source of vitamin A but the young, elderly, and pregnant should not eat raw or lightly cooked eggs to avoid salmonella.

VITAMIN A

A fat-soluble vitamin that occurs in two forms: retinol (from animal sources only) and pro-vitamin A (from animal and plant sources). Retinol is thought to be the most potent form, the form that is most readily absorbed by the body. It requires fats and minerals to be properly absorbed. Carotenes are often also mentioned along with vitamin A as they can be converted into retinol by the body.

Other names: Retinol.

Best natural source: Food from animal sources, liver, cheese, eggs, oily fish.

RDA: EC RDA: 800µg; USA RDA: 1500µg; UK RNI men: 700µg, women: 600µg.
Maximum regular daily intake should not exceed 7500µg (women) and 9000µg (men).
Maximum safe level for self supplementation 2300µg (1000RE).

Essential for: Normal growth, formation of teeth and bones, cell structure, night vision, protecting the mucus linings of the respiratory, digestive, and urinary tracts against infection. It is a component of the eye pigment visual purple.

Uses: Compounds known as retinoids have been investigated for their ability to inhibit the growth of certain types of tumor. Some drug derivatives of vitamin A are used in the treatment of severe acne and skin conditions, such as psoriasis. When applied externally it can help in the removal of age spots, impetigo, boils, carbuncles, and open ulcers. High-level use should always be under the control of a doctor.

Supplements: Usually available in two forms, in fish oils or in water dispersible forms. It is usually the type synthesized from vegetable sources (that is therefore suitable for vegetarians) that is found in

Meat and fish are an excellent source of vitamin A as well as essential fatty acids.

multivitamins. In water dispersible forms it may appear as a compound palmitate or acetate—the more stable forms—in the ingredients but this does not change the efficacy of the supplement. It should not be taken with mineral oil.

Vitamin A works best in conjunction with vitamins B complex, D, E, and minerals calcium, phosphorus, and zinc. Zinc is particularly required by the liver to release vitamin A from storage.

Deficiency: Night blindness, xeropthalmia.

Deficiency of Vitamin A is rare in developed countries. In most cases it is due to a failure to absorb sufficient amounts. Malabsorption may be due to damage in the gut, cystic fibrosis, or obstruction of the bile duct. Taken over the long-term, lipid lowering (cholesterol reducing) drugs may cause a deficiency. In less developed countries, deficiency may be due to low dietary levels of retinol and fat.

Symptoms of night blindness are characterized first by the inability to see in dim light, followed by dryness and inflammation of the eyes, and eventually blindness. Deficiency is also shown by a reduced ability to fight infections, dry rough skin, or stunted growth in children.

32

VITAMINS

Excess: Symptoms of excess or toxic amounts include headache, nausea, loss of appetite, peeling skin, and, in women, irregular menstruation. In extreme cases hair loss, rashes, blurred vision, bone pain, and fatigue may also be present.

Prolonged and excessive intake of vitamin A can result in hypervitaminosis A. It usually occurs after taking large quantities of self prescribed vitamin supplements, but interestingly it is most often seen in children. Intracranial pressure is increased and there are characteristic bone changes that can be easily seen on X-ray examination. There is high level of vitamin A in blood plasma.

Surplus vitamin A is usually stored in the liver, so it does not need daily replenishment. In extreme cases, when there are very high levels of vitamin A that is excess to requirement, the liver and spleen are enlarged. Pregnant women are warned that excessive intake may result in birth defects, and are advised not to eat liver.

CAROTENE
An orange pigment found in various colored plants.

Other names: Beta carotene.
Best natural source: Green vegetables, tomatoes, oranges, plums, peaches, and carrots.

Red, yellow, and orange fruits are great sources of beta carotene.

33

Getting a tan is fraught with vitamin danger: skin synthesis of vitamin D will slow down, and protective measures are essential. Beta carotene supplements taken before and during tanning will afford some protection but high factor sunscreens are essential for long-term skin survival.

RDA: No RDA exists; 2–5mg would be average intake from food; some nutritionists recommend 10–15mg for optimum health.

Essential for: Can be converted to vitamin A. 1mg beta carotene converts to 167µg vitamin A. Acts on its own as an antioxidant (see chapter three). Beta carotene is thought to play a part in protecting the skin from sun damage and photoaging from UV light.

Uses: Research indicates it may have a protective effect against certain types of cancer. High dietary intake may be essential for preventing cancer and a reduced risk of heart attack. Supplements may be useful for smokers and people who don't eat enough fruit and vegetables.

Supplements: These are either synthesized or made from microalgae extracts. The algae extracts are thought to be more readily absorbed and utilized by the body but tend to be more expensive. Taking a supplement prior to and for the duration of a holiday will help protect your skin but will not protect from sunburn—you need a high factor sunscreen to do that. Beta carotene is available in either multivitamin or antioxidant formulations and may sometimes be labeled in terms of its vitamin A equivalency; 15mg beta carotene would equate to 2500µg (8325IU) vitamin A.

Deficiency: Not known (but unlikely to cause a problem).

Excess: Too many carrots can cause the skin to go an orange color, especially palms and soles. Known as carrotenemia it is harmless and vanishes when the diet is altered. High intake of beta carotene supplements may increase the risk of cancer in smokers.

B COMPLEX

Pork is a rich source of a range of B vitamins, and lean meat contains a little more than beef.

The B complex of vitamins are variously described as six or eight water-soluble vitamins; biotin (also known as vitamin H) and pantothenic acid (B5) are not always included. The B vitamins all work together for body maintenance, food digestion, and development of a healthy nervous system. Nerve tissue has a high energy demand, and is particularly sensitive to shortages of B vitamins which can occur at times of stress. B1, B2, and B3 are essential to the cell's energy releasing cycle. Some of the B vitamins are closely involved with the body's defense system; all play some role in the immune system. Eyes and mouth can suffer if B vitamins are deficient; mouth ulcers have been connected with low B vitamin status.

Some people require more of the B complex than others, particularly when B vitamins have been depleted due to the effects of smoking, alcoholism, sickness, and/or stress. Research indicates that ingesting large quantities of folic acid, B6, and B12 will prevent high levels of the hormone homocysteine arising, a substance which is a risk factor in heart disease and strokes.

Most B complex supplements will provide 100 percent of the RDA for each vitamin, and these preparations will make up for minor deficiencies in your diet. The more inclusive formulations will have all more common B complex vitamins plus choline and inositol: they tend to have the Bs in levels 1000 to 2000 percent greater than

RDA values. You should note that a sudden abundance of B vitamins can result in them being excreted straight away. Slow release preparations may be beneficial, and some high strength preparations automatically are slow release.

THIAMIN, VITAMIN B1

This water-soluble vitamin was the first to be discovered in 1926. It works synergistically with B2 and B6. It can have a mild diuretic effect and is easily destroyed by cooking. Caffeine, alcohol, food processing, estrogen drugs (HRT and the oral contraceptive pill), and sulfur drugs can also deplete the supplies. Known to have beneficial effects on the nervous system and mental outlook.

Peas are a popular source of vitamin C but also have valuable amounts of B1, B3, and beta carotene.

Other names: Thiamin pyrophosphate.

Best natural source: Wholemeal grain, wheat germ bran, enriched cereals, brown rice, pasta, liver, green vegetables, pork, fish, beans, nuts, eggs.

RDA: EC RDA: 1.4mg; USA RDA: 1.5mg; UK RNI men: 1.0mg. women: 0.8mg.

Maximum safe level for self supplementation 100mg.

Essential for: Crucial role in the actions of enzymes involved in the metabolism and utilization of carbohydrates. Ensures that the brain and nerves have enough glucose for their activities and promotes growth.

Uses: Thought to help fight seasickness, improve mental outlook, and work in the treatment of herpes zoster. It is recommended that at times of stress, disease, and when recovering from surgery, B complex vitamins should be increased.

Supplements: Usually found in conjunction with other B vitamins, and it is most effective in balanced formulas. High and low dose supplement can be found.

Deficiency: Berri beri, paralysis.

People susceptible to deficiency are the elderly on a poor diet (that is also rich in sugar and refined carbohydrates) those with hypothyroidism, malabsorption disorders, or alcohol dependence. It can occur after severe illness, major surgery, or serious injury.

Deficiency causes tiredness, irritability, loss of appetite, and disturbed sleep. When severe it may cause abdominal pain, constipation, memory impairment, and beri beri. In chronic alcoholics it may cause Wernicke-Korsakoff syndrome (a rare brain disorder resulting from malnutrition).

Beri beri is a metabolic disorder which occurs mostly in developing countries. The effect is incomplete carbohydrate digestion. There are two forms: wet and dry. Wet beri beri affects the

skeletal muscles and nerves while the dry version can cause heart
failure and lead to edema. Complete cure can be effected with
oral thiamine therapy and permanent change to the diet. In Asia
people who acquire beri beri as a consequence of a diet of pol-
ished (milled) rice can be cured by adding the rice polishings
which are high in thiamine.

Excess: No known harmful effects. Rarely excess causes symptoms
which can include herpes, tremors, edema, nervousness, rapid
heartbeat, and allergies.

RIBOFLAVIN, VITAMIN B2

Water-soluble. Amount excreted depends on body needs, but may be
accompanied by protein loss. It is destroyed by ultraviolet light, and
water, estrogen, alcohol, and sulfur drugs are natural "enemies."
Riboflavin frequently shows up as being
deficient in the American diet.

Other names: Flavin mono-nucleotide,
flavin adenine dinucleotide, vitamin G.

Best natural source: Wholemeal grain,
liver, green vegetables, milk, eggs, brewer's yeast.

RDA: EC RDA: 1.6mg; USA
RDA: 1.7mg; UK RNI men: 1.3mg;
women: 1.1mg.

No upper safe limit recommended
because excess is easily excreted in
the urine.

Maximum safe level for self supplementation 200mg.

Essential for: The enzymes involved in

Brewer's yeast or yeast extract spreads can
be beneficial additions to a diet providing a
superior source of B vitamins, iron, and many
trace elements.

39

Milk is an excellent food source for young children, rich in A, B2, and B12:
make sure preschoolers only drink whole milk.

the break down and utilization of carbohydrates, fats, and proteins; the utilization of other B vitamins; production of hormones by the adrenal glands. Benefits include healthy hair, skin, and nails, and the relief of eye fatigue. Promotes growth and reproduction.

Uses: The only established use of riboflavin is in the therapy or prevention of deficiency disease.

Supplements: Available in high and low dose supplements, but most effective when taken in B complex preparation. Supplemental intakes can cause urine to become a deep yellow/green color, and this is harmless.

Deficiency: Skin lesions.

Those susceptible to deficiency include takers of estrogen-containing contraceptive pills, tricyclic antidepressants, phenothiazine antipsycotic drugs, and those with malabsorption disorders or alcohol dependence. It can occur after severe illness, major surgery, or serious injury.

Prolonged deficiency causes chapped lips, a sore tongue, and corners of the mouth eye disorders (poor visual acuity or photophobia—light shy).

Excess: No major harmful effects; symptoms of minor excess include, numbness, itching, burning, or prickling sensations.

NIACIN, VITAMIN B3

Water-soluble. The body can manufacture its own niacin using tryptophan; however a person who is deficient in B1, B2, and B6 will not be able to do this. Uptake affected by water, sulfa drugs, alcohol, food processing, sleeping pills, and estrogen.

Other names: Nicotinic acid, niacinamide (nicotinamide).

Best natural source: Lean meat, liver, poultry, fish, legumes, nuts, cereals, whole wheat products, avocados, dates, figs, prunes.

The rise in peanut allergies has been well publicized, but peanuts are still an excellent source of many micronutrients in particular B1, B3, and B6.

RDA: EC RDA: 18mg; USA RDA: 20mg; UK RNI men: 17mg; women: 13mg.
Maximum safe level for self supplementation: 150mg.

Essential for: The enzymes involved in the break down and utilization of carbohydrates, fats, and proteins; the functioning of the nervous system; production of sex hormones and maintenance of healthy skin. It can increase circulation and blood pressure.

Uses: Can help prevent and ease the severity of migraines. In Ménière's syndrome (a disorder of the inner ear) it can reduce the effects of vertigo. In large doses nicotinic acid lowers blood lipids, and so has been used in the therapy and prevention of arteriosclerotic vascular disease.

Supplements: Niacin and niacinamide are the common forms in most preparations. Niacinamide has the least side effects, which can include flushing and itching; the flushing goes after 20 minutes and can be reduced by drinking water. Concentrations in either pill or powder are 50 to 100mg.

Deficiency Pellagra.

Most deficiency is due to malabsorption disorders and alcohol dependence. Prolonged deficiency may cause pellagra, the symptoms of which include sore and cracked skin, inflammation of the tongue and mouth, and mental disturbances. It can be fatal. Those with sun-sensitive skin may be slightly deficient.

Excess: Harmful in doses over 100mg. Over 3g a day can cause liver and kidney damage and dilation of blood vessels. Some people may be particularly sensitive to low doses and experience burning or itching skin.

Figs are tasty source of niacin that make a great snack, fresh or dried.

PANTOTHENIC ACID, VITAMIN B5

First identified in 1933 as a factor necessary for curing particular skin lesions in chicks. Water-soluble. Fairly heat resistant and survives most cooking processes, but is sensitive to acid (i.e. vinegar) and alkali (i.e. bicarbonate) and easily lost in cooking water. Destroyed by canning, caffeine, sleeping pills, estrogen, alcohol, and sulfur drugs. It can be synthesized in the body by intestinal bacteria. Widely available and recognized as an anti-stress vitamin.

Zucchini (courgettes) are great either raw or cooked.

Other names: Calcium pantothenate, panthenol (*panthos* means everywhere in Greek).

All mushroom varieties are great sources of B2, niacin folate, and pantothenic acid.

Best natural source: Meat, vegetables, whole grains, wheat germ, bran, offal, brewer's yeast, nuts, chicken.

RDA: EC RDA: 6mg; USA RDA: 10mg;

Maximum safe level for self supplementation 500mg.

Essential for: The enzymes involved in metabolism of carbohydrates and fats; production of corticosteroids and sex hormones; utilization of other vitamins, functioning of nervous system, adrenal glands, and normal growth and development. Required for the synthesis of antibodies and for the utilization of PABA and choline. A constituent of coenzyme A, which plays an important part of the cell energy-releasing cycle.

Uses: It aids wound healing and post-operative shock. It can reverse the side effects of many antibiotics and prevent fatigue. It can be useful to take a supplement to provide defense against stressful situations. Cortisone, a hormone produced by the adrenal glands that helps us cope with stress, requires B5 for its formation. Some rheumatoid arthritis sufferers use it because of the mild anti-inflammatory effects of cortisone, and have reported noticeable reduction in the degree of pain and stiffness on taking B5.

Supplements: Found in B complex supplements, strengths are usually from 10 to 100mg. Doses 10 to 300mg daily. Individual supplements of pantothenic acid are the most potent. Strengths of around 100–500mg are available. As with other water-soluble vitamins, a slow release formula is probably the most effective.

Deficiency: Rare or unclear. Deficiency can occur as the result of malabsorption disorders, and as the result of severe illness, major surgery, or serious injury. The effects are fatigue, headache, nausea, abdominal pain, numbness and tingling, and muscle cramps. Severe cases may cause peptic ulcer.

Excess: No known harmful effects.

One of the most popular meat sources of protein, chicken also provides B3, B6, and B5 with a handful of useful minerals.

PYRIDOXINE, VITAMIN B6

Water-soluble and readily excreted eight hours after ingestion. B6 is actually a group of related compounds that function together. It is sometimes known as the anti-depression vitamin.

B6 is sensitive to alkalis and sunlight. Long storage, particularly canning, roasting or stewing meat, food processing, alcohol, and estrogen will all affect B6 status.

Other names: Pyridoxine, pyridoxinal, pyrodoxamine.
Best natural source: Liver, chicken, pork, fish, whole grain cereal, wheat germ, potatoes, bananas.
RDA: EC RDA: 2mg; USA RDA: 2mg; UK RNI men: 1.4mg; women: 1.2mg.
Maximum safe level for self supplementation: 200mg.

Fish isn't to everyone's fancy. It provides a comprehensive range of nutrients and is a useful low fat source of protein.

Essential for: The enzymes and hormones involved in the break down and utilization of carbohydrates, proteins, and fats; production of red blood cells and antibodies; functioning of nervous and digestive systems, and maintenance of healthy skin. Involved in the production of B3 from tryptophan and needed for the utilization of proteins.

Required for the production of serotonin, a brain chemical that affects behavior, mood, and sleep patterns. Pregnant and breast feeding women should have a higher intake.

Uses: Doses of 50–200mg are said to be helpful in relieving symptoms of premenstrual syndrome (PMS). A dose of 100mg to 2g has shown to be effective in reducing symptoms of carpel tunnel syndrome (inflammation of the nerve that passes through the wrist).

Supplements: Often incorporated in multivitamin supplements at a low level. Higher level formulations are available of strength 50–500mg and may be slow release. Those aimed at PMS sufferers often include magnesium as well.

To prevent deficiencies in other B vitamins, B6 should be taken in equal amounts with B1 and B2.

High levels B6 should not be taken by Parkinson's disease sufferers on levodopa, except under the advice of their personal medical practitioner.

Deficiency: Skin disorders, anemia, kidney stones.

Along with people with a bad diet, malabsorption disorders, those people being treated with certain drugs such as penicillamine and isoniazid can suffer from a deficiency. A deficiency may

*Bananas are rich in B6 and vitamin C. They are a
useful source of potassium and manganese too.*

cause depression, irritability, weakness, skin disorders, inflamed mouth and tongue, cracked lips, anemia, and in infants, seizures. Women on the oral contraceptive pill may have low levels which can lead to mild depression.

In susceptible people, deficiency can lead to kidney stone formation.

Excess: Intake of over 100 times RDA (2–10g) can cause neuritis (inflammation of a nerve). It is also said to play a part in night restlessness and vivid dream recall.

FOLIC ACID

This is a water-soluble compound that can be destroyed by over cooking. Many foods are fortified with folic acid, in particular cereals and bread.

PABA (para-amino-benzoic acid) is part of the structure of folic acid but does not have any action on its own. However, it is often

found in sunscreens and can be used in the treatment of vitiligo (with high oral doses). PABA is sometimes added to B complex groupings and listed separately.

Other names: Folacin, folate, pteroylglutamic acid, vitamin M.

RDA: EC RDA: 200µg; USA RDA: 400µg; UK RNI men: 200µg, women: 200µg.

Spinach, Popeye's favorite food, is rich in folates and antioxidants.

Maximum safe level for self
supplementation 400µg.

Best natural source: Liver, leafy
green vegetables, legumes,
yeast, whole grain cereals,
nuts, egg yolks.

Essential for: Vital for manufacture of nucleic acids and
growth and reproduction.
Also required for the production of red blood cells and
proper functioning of the
nervous system.

Uses: It is recommended that
women trying to become
pregnant take additional

*As with other nuts, cashews are a rich supply of
micronutrients, in particular folate, B1, and B3.*

folic acid and continue to do so for the first 12 weeks after conception to prevent neural tube defects (such as spina bifida).

Supplements: It appears in B complex and multivitamin preparations
at levels of 50–200µg. Not really taken separately except during
pregnancy; most single supplements have levels of 400µg. Single
supplements may also include other useful nutrients like B12, iron,
calcium, or fish oils which are all recognized as being helpful to
both mother and fetus during pregnancy.

Folic acid supplements should not be taken with epilepsy drugs
except on medical advice.

Deficiency: Anemia (rare).

Mild deficiency is quite common but easily corrected by a
change of diet. Severe deficiency can occur during pregnancy or
breast feeding, in premature babies, people undergoing dialysis,
people with certain blood disorders, psoriasis, malabsorption

disorders, alcohol dependents, and those taking certain drugs including antimalarial drugs, anticonvulsant drugs, estrogen-containing oral contraceptives, corticosterosids, sulfonamides drugs, and some analgesics. Primary effects are anemia, soreness around the mouth, and poor growth in children.

Excess: Not really known, although some people can experience allergic skin reactions. In rare cases high doses have been known to mask a deficiency of B12. B12 deficiency results in the same type of anemia and folic acid may cure this but not any nervous damage which may go undetected. High levels may affect the level zinc that is absorbed.

Neural tube defects occur when the vertebrae—the bones surrounding the spine—fail to form properly and don't fuse as they should during early fetal development. During early pregnancy, folic acid, with the help of B12, is essential for precise cell formation and growth. There is much scientific research that has shown conclusively that folic acid, if taken prior to conception and during early pregnancy, will prevent women having babies with these types of defect.

Women who have already had one baby with a neural tube defect need much more than the recommended 400μg dose if they are planning another pregnancy and medial advice must be sought.

BIOTIN

Water-soluble, organic compound that contains sulfur.
Reputedly aids in keeping hair from turning gray, is helpful for the preventative treatment of baldness, and can
alleviate dermatitis. Its enemies include food processing
methods, alcohol, water, sulfur drugs, and estrogen. It works
synergistically with vitamins A, B2 (riboflavin), B6, and B3 (niacin).

Other names: Coenzyme R, vitamin H.

Best natural source: Widespread: liver, peanuts, dried
beans, egg yolk, mushrooms, bananas, grapefruit, watermelon; synthesized by intestinal bacteria.

RDA: Maximum safe level for self supplementation: 0.5g.

Essential for: Required for the activities of enzymes
involved with fatty acid and carbohydrate metabolism
plus for the excretion of waste products of protein
break down. It can be synthesized by intestinal bacteria.

Uses: Single biotin supplements are sometimes taken by people with
the fungal infection *Candia albicans*. It is thought to slow the rate of

*Grapefruit is good for
those recovering from
illness, but should not
be eaten if you are
taking certain
antihistamines such as
(triludan).*

growth of the gut organism,
preventing it developing into
the more invasive from of
infection of the bloodstream.

Supplements Generally found as
part of B complex
preparations, although single
supplements are available at
doses of 25 to 300µg.

Deficiency: Rare, even in people
on restricted diets. May occur
during treatment with antibiotic

drugs or sulfonamide drugs. It can develop after long-term consumption of raw eggs or egg whites which interfere with biotin absorption.

Symptoms include weakness, tiredness, poor appetite, hair loss, depression, an inflamed tongue, and eczema.

Excess: No known harmful effects.

Watermelon always looks mouthwateringly delicious, so it's nice to know eating it provides essential elements of our diet too.

VITAMIN B12

Water-soluble. Its function is closely related to folic acid and both are involved in the production of new cells, particularly new red blood cells. It is the only vitamin to contain essential minerals (cobalt) as part of its chemical structure. It needs to be absorbed with calcium in order to obtain the maximum benefit to the body. It is adversely affected by acids and alkalis, sunlight, alcohol, estrogen, water, and sleeping pills.

Other names: Cyanocobalamin, cobalamin, antipernicious factor, the red vitamin.

Best natural source: Liver, kidney, eggs, fish, milk and other dairy products, brewer's yeast, fortified soya products, fortified breakfast cereals.

RDA: EC RDA: 1µg; USA RDA: 6µg; UK RNI men: 1.5µg, women: 1.5µg.
   Maximum safe level for self supplementation 500µg.

Essential for: Vital role in the activities of several enzymes. Also in the production of genetic material, so it is essential for growth and development; also production of red blood cells and the utilization of folic acid.

Uses: Mainly the treatment of deficiency disease. Treatment for pernicious anemia is by injection as oral supplements are not suitable. For vegetarian or vegans a modest supplement will correct mild deficiency. Women may find it useful as part of a B complex formula, just prior to menstruation. Can improve memory, concentration, balance, and relieve irritability.

Supplements: Usually a component of multivitamins although it can be purchased as a separate supplement. Typical dose is 10µg, but they vary quite widely. It is not absorbed well through the stomach, and therefore slow release formulas may work best (and will be absorbed in the intestine). Most supplements are made by

Seafood, in particular shellfish, is one of many sources of B12.

fermentation of animal products, so some formulations may not be suitable for vegetarians or vegans. Spirulina, chlorella, and other algae type supplements also provide B12 in amounts commensurate with the RDA.

Deficiency: Pernicious anemia.

Deficiency is due to the inability of the intestine to absorb the vitamin, commonly as a result of pernicious anemia. B12 absorption is reliant on a compound—a glycoprotein—called intrinsic factor secreted in gastric juices in the small intestine. In people who are deficient or not producing this factor, the result is pernicious anemia. The disease can run in families and can be the consequence of an abnormal immune response which damages the apparatus for making intrinsic factor. The result is fewer, irregular blood cells. In the longer term, if it is not treated the effects are not reversible.

Deficiency can occur after gastrectomy (removal of part of the stomach) or as a result of malabsorption disorders. It can be missing from vegetarian and vegan diets. Main symptoms include sore mouth and tongue and damage to spinal cord, resulting in tingling and numbness in limbs. Occasionally slight memory loss and depression occur too.

Excess: No known harmful effects.

OTHER COMPONENTS IN B COMPLEX

Choline and inositol are not B vitamins but are important factors which complement the B complex and are sometimes included in B complex supplements. They both have a function in the liver in the metabolism of fat. Choline is used to form part of the molecule acetyl choline, an important neurotransmitter in the brain. For more information see the section on lipotropics.

VITAMIN C

Water-soluble. Vitamin C is readily lost in food processing, cooking, and while keeping foods warm.

As well as having many useful properties vitamin C is a powerful antioxidant and works with vitamin E to protect the outer parts of cells. It can prevent cholesterol from becoming oxidized, which can be the first stage prior to the "furring" of arteries.

Other names: Ascorbic acid.

Best natural source: Fresh fruit: citrus fruits, strawberries, and blackcurrants are potent sources. Also tomatoes, green leafy vegetables, especially green capsicums, Brussels sprouts, and potatoes. A 200ml glass of freshly squeezed orange juice contains around 80mg of vitamin C.

RDA: EC RDA: 60mg; USA RDA: 60mg; UK RNI 40mg. Smokers may need more: 80mg. Some people feel the full antioxidant effect is only effective at 150–200mg. Maximum safe level for self supplementation 2000mg.

Essential for: Activities of various enzymes. Vital for the manufacture of collagen, which is necessary for the growth and repair of tissues, gums, teeth, and blood vessels, growth and maintenance of healthy bones and ligaments. Needed for the production of

Orange juice is one of the most popular ways to get your daily dose of vitamin C.

Above and overleaf: Strawberries are a nutritious and
delicious source of vitamin C.

certain neurotransmitters (brain chemicals), adrenal gland hormones; used in the response to healing.

Required for the absorption of iron from non-meat sources so is useful to vegetarians or those prone to anemia.

Uses: Many people take very large doses of supplements to prevent the common cold—it can reduce the length and severity of a cold, although it may not prevent us catching a cold in the first place.

It is known to boost the immune system because it acts to strengthen the action of white blood cells that are in the first line of defense against bacteria and viruses.

It has mild antihistamine properties and may be useful to hayfever or mild allergy sufferers. High intakes are linked to lower rates of stomach cancer. Smokers, drinkers, and people working in polluted areas can also benefit from extra vitamin C in their diet.

If you are under particular physical or mental stress, vitamin C will be lost from the adrenal glands, and it is thought that it plays a role in the production of corticosteroid hormones such as cortisone.

Supplements: One of the most widely available and taken supplements. Available in a variety of strengths and preparations. If you are just boosting dietary levels taking the RDA value is probably best. For more specific effects aim for a higher

Along with strawberries, blackcurrants are one of the richest sources of vitamin C and also provide a valuable anticancer antioxidant lutein.

daily dose of 1000mg. It should be noted however that you do not absorb all of the vitamin C that you take. Daily intakes of 150mg are 80 to 95 percent absorbed; doses of 1500mg are only about 50 percent absorbed.

The most efficacious supplements contain vitamin C and the bioflavonoids rutin and hesperidin (sometimes labeled as citrus salts). These supplements are thought to enhance the absorption of vitamin C—supplements with "patented" vitamin C seem to offer no extra benefits.

Deficiency: Scurvy. Deficiency is rare; slight deficiency may occur as the result of a serious injury or burn, major surgery, use of oral contraceptive, fever, or inhalation of carbon monoxide. Symptoms of mild deficiency include weakness, general aches and pains,

The US chemist (and Nobel Prize winner) Linus Pauling (1901–94) was infamous primarily for two reasons: first he was a controversial member and active campaigner of the peace movement in the USA in the 1950s and 60s; second he was passionate in his advocacy of vitamin C. He was convinced it was efficacious in combating a wide range of illnesses and diseases. Pauling was an advocate of the "megavitamin theory" which took off in the 1950s after psychiatrists Humphrey Osmond and Abraham Hoffer used the term to describe the very large does of niacin they prescribed to treat schizophrenia. The medical community at large has not approved the megavitamin theory. Pauling's views generated a lot of controversy, but in the end no firm scientific proof.

The average orange provides about 60mg of vitamin C, adequate to meet your RDA.

swollen gums, and nosebleeds. Severe deficiency leads to scurvy and anemia.

Most animals can synthesize their own sources but we can't. Some people are predisposed to scurvy because they do not have an enzyme that is required for ascorbic acid. Typical to this disorder are fragile capillaries (very small blood vessels) and it can lead to internal bleeding, degeneration of cartilage, loosening of teeth, joint and bone pain.

Excess: Not usually harmful when taken to excess unless dose is more than 1 mg. Excess can cause diarrhea, nausea, stomach cramps, and occasionally kidney stones.

It should not be used by cancer patients undergoing radiation or chemotherapy and high levels of supplementation are not advisable for those with poor kidney function.

VITAMIN D

Fat-soluble and acquired through sunlight or diet. We can manufacture it when UV light acts on the cholesterol in the skin to produce the vitamin, but this process ceases once a tan is established. Dark skinned people also have difficulty synthesizing it.

As it is manufactured by one organ (the skin) and has an effect on other organs (intestines and bones) it is technically a hormone. It requires fats to be properly absorbed. It must first pass through the liver and kidneys before it can be used.

Irradiation of food products with UV light increases their vitamin D content.

Other names: Collective name for several compounds including ergocalciferol (D2), cholecalciferol (D3).

61

You can obtain a range of fat-soluble
vitamins and minerals from oily fish.

Best natural source: Fish
liver oils, sardines, herring,
mackerel, salmon, tuna,
liver, egg yolk; some synthesized in the skin.

RDA: EC RDA: 5µg; USA
RDA: 10µg; UK RNI: no
recommendation for non-
pregnant adult under 65.
Children and the elderly
are likely to need more,
while most healthy adults
can manufacture sufficient
amounts.

Maximum safe level for
self supplementation
10µg (400IU).

Essential for: Regulation of the levels of calcium and phosphate in
the body, which are critical for correct nerve function; aids absorption of calcium from the intestine and required for strong bones
and teeth.

Uses: Used in the treatment of osteoporosis (a disease that causes
brittle bones) because its role in regulating calcium and phosphorus is essential for bones and teeth. Babies are sometimes
prescribed drops to help with bone formation.

Supplements: D2 is manufactured from yeast organisms and it is
suitable for vegetarians although some preparations may contain
animal gelatin. D3 is the form that is found naturally in animal food
sources. Interestingly it is manufactured from the cholesterol
content of lanolin and this is obtained from the wool of
living sheep.

62

Many people take vitamin D as part of a cod liver oil formulation, which frequently also contains vitamin A.

Deficiency: Rickets, osteomalacia, lack of absorption of calcium in the gut.

Deficiency may occur in people with a poor diet, premature infants, those deprived of sunlight (night workers and people living in northern climates or areas with short daylight hours), dark skinned people, particularly if they live in smoggy or urban areas where they cannot absorb enough UV light rays. Occasionally lactating women and those whose religious beliefs require them to keep their skin covered may also be affected. Research has shown that adequate exposure to the sun of the cheeks can be enough to synthesize the daily requirement of vitamin D in European infants. Deficiency occurs with certain intestinal absorption disorders; also with liver disease, kidney disorders, and some genetic defects. Prolonged use of some drugs (phenytoin—an anticonvulsant) may cause deficiency.

Osteomalcia is uncommon in developed countries although it can accompany osteoporosis in old age. Rickets still occurs in children, particularly in those of Asian origin. Rickets is characterized by bow legs, but can also be seen by deformities of rib cage and skull.

Excess: Upsets the balance of calcium and phosphate in the body and leads to hypercalcemia (high levels of calcium in the blood). Symptoms include weakness, abnormal thirst, increased urination, gastrointestinal disturbances, and depression. Excess may lead to abnormal calcium deposits in the tissues, kidneys, and blood vessels. In children it may lead to the slowing down or stopping of growth. Prolonged dietary intakes of 50µg per day could cause mild symptoms.

Less expensive and more widely available nowadays, salmon has
become more commonplace in the supermarket and on the dinner plate.
It is a good source of B1, B3, B6, B12, D, and E vitamins.

VITAMIN E

Originally hailed as an aphrodisiac because it was discovered to be a factor in rat fertility, it has not proved to have the same effect in humans. (It should be noted that vitamins for one species might not be essential in another or work in precisely the same way.) However, it is important to other aspects of health; it's a powerful antioxidant and is thought to have a protective affect against aging.

It is fat-soluble and is stored in the liver and fatty tissues of the body as well as heart, muscles, testes, uterus, blood, adrenals, and pituitary glands. Our intake varies according to the amount of polyunsaturated fats we eat: the higher the level, the more vitamin E we require. It can be destroyed by heat, freezing temperatures, food processing, oxygen, iron, and choline.

Other names: Actually a group of about eight tocopherols that are distinguished by Greek alphabet designation: alpha, beta, gamma, delta, epsilon, seta, eta, theta. D-alpha tocopherol is most important.

Best natural source: It occurs in small amounts in a wide range of foods. Vegetables oils, whole grain cereals, nuts, leafy green vegetables, wheat germ, avocados, blackberries, asparagus, egg yolks.

RDA: EC RDA: 10mg; USA RDA: 10mg; UK RNI: 5mg.
Maximum safe level for self supplementation 800mg.

Asparagus in a nut dressing certainly provides a plateful of vitamin E.

Squid looks more appetizing when cooked! Even so it's a good source of vitamins B3, B6, B12, and E, as well as minerals selenium and iodine.

Essential for: Normal cell structure, and maintaining activities of enzymes and formation of red blood cells. Protects lungs and other tissues from damage by pollutants and is believed to slow aging process of cells. Tocopherols are concerned with protecting fats from oxidation within the body.

Uses: Vitamin E is frequently found in skin lotions and beauty creams as it is thought to improve dry skin. It is also thought to help prevent thick scar formation. Some women find single supplements useful in alleviating the symptoms of PMS or during the hot flushes of menopause.

Vitamin E seems to show promise as a good preventative treatment against heart attacks. In one US study users of supplements of 67mg (100IU) had significantly reduced risks.

Supplements: Often part of multivitamin preparations at levels suitable for those who do not get enough through their food. Single supplements are usually oil based capsules although some dry formulations can be found and these may be more appropriate for vegans, vegetarians, and those who cannot absorb fat properly.

Vitamin E is the only vitamin that is less active in its synthetic form. When derived from natural sources such as soya oil, it will be called d-alpha tocopherol and this is the more potent form. Its synthetic form dl-alpha tocopherol shows less biological activity. In addition it may also be listed as acetate or succinate but this does not alter is efficacy.

Deficiency: Rare. Usually occurs as a result of malabsorption disorders, with certain liver disorders and in premature infants. Deficiency leads to destruction of red blood cells resulting in anemia in infants, irritability, and edema. Deficiency has been shown to cause infertility in rats, and liver dysfunction.

Excess: Unusually for a fat-soluble vitamin, it is very safe. Prolonged excessive intake (over 800mg) can cause abdominal pain, nausea, diarrhea, and vomiting. It may reduce the absorption of vitamins A, D, K, and in severe cases cause deficiency in those vitamins.

A staple for many salads and sauces, fresh tomatoes are rich in vitamins C, E, and beta carotene.

Eggplants are a good source of a range of vitamins, but only K in significant quantities.

VITAMIN K

Fat-soluble. It is can be manufactured by bacteria that live in the intestine. It is destroyed by x-rays, radiation, pollution in the air, aspirin, and frozen foods.

Other names: Phylloquinone (natural plant source), menadione (synthetic form).

Best natural source: Fish oils, leafy green vegetables, especially cabbage, broccoli, turnip greens, alfalfa, eggplant (aubergine), vegetable oils, yogurt, egg yolks, cheese, pork, and liver.

RDA: None set as deficiency so rare. Intake of 300µg considered adequate.

Essential for: Formation in the liver of substances, primarily prothrombin, that promote blood clotting.

Uses: Some deficient newborn babies are given vitamin K at birth.

Supplements: As it is so abundant in food sources, supplementation is unnecessary.

Deficiency: Deficiency is rare as most adults can synthesize it. Blood clotting disorders are the main problem as deficiency reduces the ability of blood to clot which

Mainly a supply of vitamins A and B12, most cheeses contain small amounts of vitamin K too.

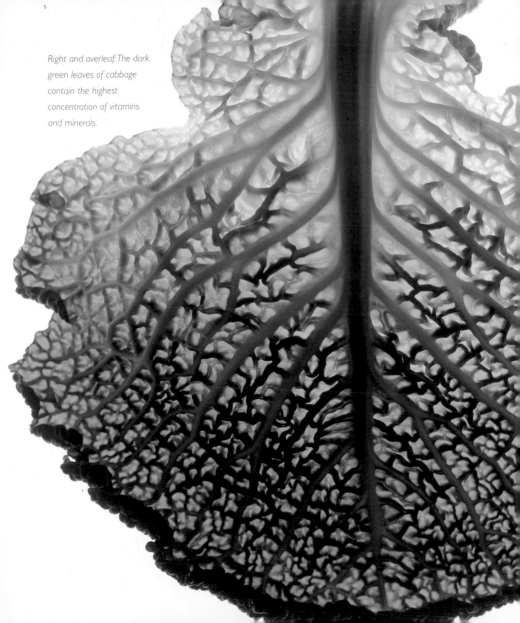

Right and overleaf: The dark green leaves of cabbage contain the highest concentration of vitamins and minerals.

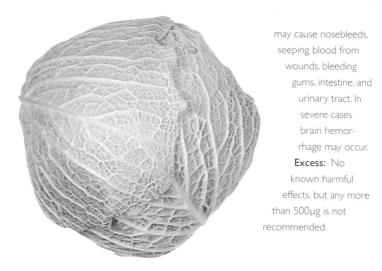

may cause nosebleeds, seeping blood from wounds, bleeding gums, intestine, and urinary tract. In severe cases brain hemorrhage may occur. **Excess:** No known harmful effects, but any more than 500µg is not recommended.

LESSER KNOWN VITAMINS

The following is a list of little known compounds that have been called vitamins, and research is still being carried out on most of them.

• **Vitamin B10 and B11** are additional names for a collection of growth factors.

• **Vitamin F** is a collective term for the unsaturated linoleic, linolenic, and arachidonic fatty acids. Unsaturated fats aid the metabolism of saturated fat, and it's a good idea to include them if you have a heavy carbohydrate intake. They can be found in vegetables oils, almonds, avocados, peanut, pecans, and sunflower seeds. More will be said about these compounds in the chapter on lipotropics.

• **Vitamin L** is a factor that is needed for lactation.

• **Vitamin B13:** Orotic acid has been designated B13, but so little is known about it no RDA has been established. Its best dietary sources are root vegetables and whey. It is easily destroyed by sunlight and water. It is essential for the metabolism of folic acid and B12. Calcium orotate is used in supplements.

• **Vitamin B15:** Pangamic acid is water-soluble and it works as an antioxidant like vitamin E. Not approved by the USA FDA, it has been approved for use in Russia, where the bulk of research has been carried out. It is not strictly a vitamin as it has not been proved to be necessary

Pecans are a useful supplier of vitamin F as well
as the all important monounsaturated fats.

We all know carrots are great for beta carotene and vitamin C,
but this root vegetable also contains small amounts of orotic acid too.

to human diet and health. It has several reported benefits including neutralizing alcohol cravings (and so is good at staving off hangovers), and protecting the liver from cirrhosis; lowers blood cholesterol levels; relieves the symptoms of angina and asthma; and can boost recovery from fatigue. It is found in brewer's yeast, whole grains, brown rice, and pumpkin and sesame seeds.

Research indicates that initial supplementation can cause nausea unless taken after the main meal of the day. Maximum daily supplementation should not exceed 150mg.

Brimming with bioflavinoids, cherries contain ellagic acid, which may work as an anticancer agent, and anthocyanins which can relieve pain.

• **Vitamin B17** is a controversial vitamin, officially the compound amygdalin, but also called laetrile; it is known as nitrilosides by medics. It has not received FDA approval because of its cyanide content, but it is reputed to have cancer controlling and preventative actions. It is found naturally in apricot, apple, cherry, plum, peach, and nectarine kernels. I wouldn't recommend that anyone takes it, but it is certainly one to watch out for.

Nectarines and apricots offer a snack packed with vitamin C and potassium, but we don't normally eat the kernel.

• **Vitamin P** is a term used for a variety of bioflavonoids; alternatively known as C complex (because they work with vitamin C synergistically), citrus bioflavonoids, rutin and hesperidin. We will look at these compounds in the chapter on antioxidants. They are sometimes called capillary permeability factors as they strengthen the walls of capillaries and help to prevent bruising. They are found in pith (the white skin) of citrus fruits and in apricots, blackberries, buckwheat, cherries, and rosehip.

• **Vitamin T and U**—very little is known about these compounds. Vitamin T is known to help blood coagulation and platelet formation (platelets are "broken" bits of blood cells essential for wound repair). It is reputedly useful in treatment of anemia and hemophilia but it is not widely available. It is found in egg yolks and sesame seeds.

Vitamin U has been extracted from raw cabbage juice and medical opinions vary as to its uses. It might be useful in the healing of ulcers.

As well as a potential source of vitamin B17, plums contain a fair amount or fiber and beta carotene.

2. MINERALS

What are minerals?

Minerals are inorganic substances that along with vitamins are essential micronutrients for a healthy functioning body. At least 20 mineral elements are essential to our diet with the most important being calcium, magnesium, phosphorus, potassium, and sodium. Others, such as copper, iron, and zinc, are needed in such small quantities that they are frequently called trace elements.

Many of the minerals are metals that in nature exist as salts (a type of chemical compound) and it is these that are used in supplements. The mineral salts can be either inorganic (carbonates, chlorides, oxides, and sulfates) or organic (compounds that contain carbon and are called citrates, fumerates, gluconates, and lactates). Generally it is the organic versions which are more readily absorbed and also better tolerated by the body. If the mineral salt is soluble, the free mineral will be released on reaching the intestine and then be absorbed. However, some components of foods, such as substances found in high fiber foods (called phytates i.e. phytic acid), can latch on to the mineral and block its absorption, and the minerals are more likely to be excreted rather than utilized.

What do minerals do?

We need minerals for normal management of our bodies and body systems. They are essential components of our teeth and bones (calcium,

Left: Most people eat pistachios, little realizing how packed with essential minerals they are.

phosphorus, and magnesium), they help to regulate body fluids (sodium, potassium, and chlorine) and they are components of enzymes and hormones which regulate body functions, especially the nervous system. While minerals can generally be found in the majority of foods, we don't always eat the right balance to ensure we get sufficient quantities to satisfy our body's metabolic needs. This can happen at times of growth, stress, trauma, blood loss, and as a result of some diseases. Our mineral requirements are unique to each individual and will depend on our age, sex, and lifestyle.

As children, our need for many minerals is greater than it is as an adult; growth is an energy and nutrient dependent activity.

It's all in the ground

Minerals are found in varying quantities in our foods and drinks but where do they come from originally? All plants absorb minerals from the soil, which they use for similar reasons to us (growth and development, regulation of processes, constituents of enzymes). To get access to the minerals we must either consume the plants or animals that have eaten the plants. However, one reason that the amount of minerals vary in our diets, no matter how constant or varied our choice of foods, is that animals and plants are dependent upon the soil in which the plants are grown. The composition of soil will vary across different areas, as anyone who has watched a gardening program on TV will know, and is dependent on the type of bedrock on which the soil rests. As well as the size of the soil particles (which has an impact on drainage), soil can be acid or alkali, and the type of plants that will grow in it will depend on their nutrient preference.

Soils can always be topped up with the missing nutrients by using fertilizer: a soil test will confirm what sort to use, organic – like manure—or inorganic—like NPK (nitrogen, phosphorus, and potassium) fertilizer. In ancient times farmers used to practice a system of crop rotation; this method meant that every few years, the farmer would make sure that he changed or alternated the crops between his various fields. The farmer would also ensure that he grew some legumes (peas, beans) in at least one field a year, which actively put nutrients—particularly nitrates—back into the soil. Over years the problems and demands of intensive farming can deplete even the healthiest of soils if something isn't put

Broad beans supply an excellent supply of a range of vitamins and minerals as well as fiber and antioxidants.

back. The result is that the crops aren't as full of all the minerals either. In areas where the soil is nutrient poor and there is consequently a risk of deficiency, food is fortified as necessary.

When do we need supplements?

It is unusual for people not to obtain the full complement of minerals from their diet, and excess may not only prove to be unbeneficial but can actually be harmful. Dietary supplements such as multivitamin preparations frequently contain a mixture of vitamins and minerals to supply the full RDA for most vitamins, but not always for minerals. Single supplements will vary and you should check the label information. Single mineral supplements are only available for a few commonly missing or required nutrients.

However, occasionally doctors do prescribe minerals supplements. Iron is the most commonly used mineral supplement, which is used to treat iron deficient anemia and is sometimes needed by women at times of pregnancy or when breast feeding. Iodine is sometimes added to salt and bread in areas where the soil is nutrient poor and there is consequently a risk of deficiency. Calcium supplements are also used during pregnancy and sometimes for young children.

Most mineral deficiencies are extremely rare, but can occur through malabsorption disorders which can occur as a result of illness or after surgery. The exception is magnesium deficiency which can occur as a result of alcohol dependence, kidney disease, or prolonged treatment with either diuretic or digitalis drugs.

What's in a name?

Many books and references to minerals mention chelated minerals, primarily because it is believed that they are better absorbed. Chelated minerals are compounds of a mineral with an organic component—like an amino acid. The idea is that the amino acid and mineral are absorbed

Most nuts will contribute significant amounts of iron, magnesium, and zinc if eaten regularly in a balanced diet.

together and that the mineral can't be "pinched" by other dietary components, and lost with body waste products. There are certain specific chelates that sometimes appear on the label of multivitamin and mineral supplements: zinc picolinate or seleno-methione and are usually the more potent compound for the mineral.

Some minerals may be yeast bound. They are produced by growing yeast organisms in a mineral enriched environment. Reputedly they are very well absorbed as a result. However, if you are on a yeast-free diet, check the labels!

As with vitamins, most minerals are listed by weight on labels. It is the case for most minerals that the organic form of the mineral is better absorbed, so look out for the organic compounds on the list of ingredients.

CALCIUM

Calcium is the most abundant mineral in the body; at any one time it makes up about a kilo of our weight and to maintain it we need to get 1g daily.

Calcium forms part of the matrix of our bones and teeth (in the form of calcium phosphate—which is why we also have a requirement for phosphorus). In addition it has many functions within the body at the level of the smallest cells. It is crucial for muscle contractions, sending the impulses along nerve fibers to the muscle and is needed for blood clotting.

Rhubarb is well known for its oxalic acid content. Small amounts are not toxic but most gardeners are careful not to eat the stalks of the first crop.

Vitamin D and two hormones—parathyroid hormone and calcitonin—work together to regulate how much is absorbed and to control the level of calcium within the body. The optimum amount of calcium carried in the blood is about 0.1 percent of the total amount in the body. If this level falls parathyroid hormone causes more to be released from the bones. When the level of calcium is too high, calcitonin counteracts and causes more to be excreted (in the urine).

You may have heard of drugs called calcium channel blockers. These are commonly used in the treatment of angina, hypertension, and arrhythmia. They work by slowing the nerve impulse which can help correct certain types of heart problems like arrhythmia.

Every day we excrete about 500mg of calcium in our urine and so we need to replace it daily. Its absorption is affected by large quantities of fat, oxalic acid (found in rhubarb and some chocolate), phytic acid found in some grains.

Chemical symbol: Ca.

RDA: EC RDA: 800mg; USA RDA: 1000mg; UK RNI 700mg.

Maximum safe level for self supplementation 1500mg.

Best natural source: All dairy products, egg fish, leafy green vegetables,

Cheese is a tasty way to get calcium, as well as a good source of B12 for non-meat eaters. Vegetarians who want to avoid animal products can find rennet-free cheese readily available in most supermarkets now.

tinned sardines, tofu, fortified soya milk, nuts particularly brazil and almonds, sunflower seeds, spinach, seaweed, dried figs, dried beans.

Essential for: Transmission of impulses along nerve fibers, muscle contractions, blood clotting. Calcium works with magnesium for cardiovascular health. It also helps the metabolism of iron and has a role in alleviating insomnia.

Uses: Calcium can help reduce irritability and mild hypertension; having a mug of warm milk at bedtime may help you sleep better. It can bring relief to menstrual cramps, some backache, and growing pains.

Supplements: Calcium supplements are sometimes taken by pregnant and breast feeding women and by growing children. Vitamin D is essential for absorption of calcium, so it is frequently included in supplements as is magnesium (which should be in a 1:2 ratio with calcium). Organic forms are best absorbed, i.e. compounds of calcium like gluconate (best for vegetarians) or lactate, amino acid chelated calcium. Calcium carbonate (chalk) may appear less bulky than some preparations but it is insoluble and is not well absorbed by those with a poor digestion. Available in 100–500mg doses.

Deficiency: Rickets, osteomalacia, and osteoporosis can result from a lack of calcium. A serious lack of calcium is known as hypocalcaemia. Abnormal levels of calcium can disrupt cell function, particularly muscles and nerves. Reduced calcium levels sometimes occur in people who suffer from insomnia.

Excess: Hypercalcaemia occurs with a substantial intake of calcium (for instance taking over 2000mg). Accumulation of calcium can result in kidney stones when normal control mechanisms are not longer working properly. Some drugs increase the blood calcium level, but excess is usually excreted.

CHLORINE

In nature chlorine is a yellowish green gas, which we all know has powerful bleaching properties. It is an irritant and inhaling large amounts can be fatal. However, it forms compounds called chlorides, the main one we know about is sodium chloride or salt.

Chemical symbol: Cl.

RDA: None established; an average dietary salt intake will provide an adequate amount.

Best natural source: Salt, kelps, olives.

If you have a craving for olives, it could be because you need more salt in your diet.

Essential for: Regulating blood acid-alkali balance, helping liver function.

Uses: Keeps you supple (a lack of salt in the diet can lead to muscle cramps) and improves digestion.

Supplements: It is included in most multivitamin and multimineral preparations.

Deficiency: Loss of hair and teeth.

Excess: Over 15mg daily can lead to nasty side effects.

CHROMIUM

A metallic element essential for the activities of several enzymes. It exists in two chemical forms, trivalent and hexavalent: the trivalent form is active as a nutrient; the hexavalent form can be toxic.

It is recommended that insulin dependent diabetics do not take single chromium supplements without a doctor's advice and guidance.

Chemical symbol: Cr.

RDA: EC RDA: 25μg; 90μg is an average intake.
Maximum safe level for self supplementation 200μg.

Best natural source: Whole grains, meat, brewer's yeast, cheese, shellfish, chicken, hard water.

Essential for: Forms part of organic complex called glucose tolerance factor (GTF) with niacin (vitamin B3) and a variety of amino acids. GTF increases the effectiveness of insulin in the regulation of blood sugar levels. It might also have a role in keeping blood cholesterol levels low.

Uses: Often taken by people who crave sugary foods to help regulate of blood sugar levels.

Supplements: Can be founding multivitamin and multimineral

Lobster is a delicious way to intake a whole host of minerals, particularly chromium.

preparations in a typical dose of 25µg but in single supplements can be found in strengths of 100 or 200µg. Chromium picolinate or chelated chromium provides the trivalent (safest) form of the mineral. Chromium yeast is thought to be rich in GTF and is particularly well absorbed by the body.

Deficiency: Rare. Severe deficiency results in poor glucose tolerance which could lead to diabetes. It is implicated in artherosclerosis (poor blood sugar control is a risk factor for the disease). A refined diet high in sugars could lead to chromium deficiency.

Excess: In excess chromium is highly toxic (poisonous) and produces inflammation of the skin. If chromium vapor (used in industrial circumstances) is inhaled it damages the nose, and can cause increased risk of cancer. There are doubts about the long-term safety of taking chromium supplements.

COBALT

A metallic element that forms part of the molecule of vitamin B12. In its radioactive form it is used in radiotherapy.

For those that don't really like shellfish, chicken or whole grains are good alternative sources of many minerals.

Chemical symbol: Co.

RDA: EC RDA: 2µg; USA RDA: 2µg; UK RNI men: 1.4µg; women: 1.2µg.

Best natural source: Meat, kidney, liver, oysters, clams, milk.

Essential for: Essential for red blood cells.

Uses: Can help ward off anemia.

Supplements: Rarely found in supplements and is best obtained from food sources.

Deficiency: Anemia. A strict vegetarian diet may lead to deficiency.

Excess: Not known.

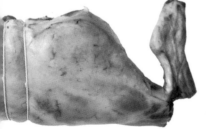

COPPER

A metallic element that is an essential component of several enzymes. Found in cigarettes, oral contraceptive pills, and pollution.

Although most meat will supply useful vitamins and minerals, lamb contains quite high levels of fat.

Chemical symbol: Cu.

RDA: EC RDA: 2mg; USA RDA: 2mg; UK RNI men: 1.4mg; women: 1.2mg.

　Maximum self supplementation dose: 5mg.

Best natural source: Whole wheat, prunes, dried beans, peas, shrimps, most seafood, liver.

Essential for: Needed for iron to be converted to hemoglobin (the red, oxygen carrying pigment in blood) and the utilization of vitamin C.

Supplements: Found in most multivitamin and mineral preparations at the maximum RDA, but it is rare that supplementation would be required if you eat enough vegetables and whole wheat.

Deficiency: Very uncommon.

Excess: Poisoning due to excess is rare but can occur when people drink homemade alcohol that has been distilled using a equipment with copper tubes. Symptoms include nausea, vomiting, and diarrhea. It may result in Wilson's disease, a rare disorder of copper metabolism. Excess is also known to lower zinc levels.

Most sea creatures absorb their minerals directly from seawater, which is why they are first-rate foods for us to eat.

FLUORINE

Like chlorine this element is usually needed by our bodies in the form of compounds, in this case they are called fluorides. In this form it is useful in helping to prevent dental decay because it helps to strengthen the outer layer of teeth, the enamel. It may also play a role in reducing the ability of acid-producing microorganisms in the mouth to produce plaque (which in turn can lead to tooth decay). Fluorine is frequently added to water (and toothpaste) to help improve the strength of teeth. Children who drink fluoridate water from birth have fewer cavities and extractions than children who have low fluoride intakes.

Gelatin can be present in many foods, but is derived from animals so vegetarians should check labels of commercial products such as mousses, moulds, and some fruit yogurts.

Chemical symbol: F.

RDA: None established.

Best natural source: Fluoridated drinking water, seafood, gelatin.

Essential for: Dental health and strengthening bones.

Supplements: Not found in supplements.

Deficiency: Tooth decay.

Excess: Called fluorosis this can cause the tooth enamel to become spotted, and if severe the enamel can become brown-stained. Cases only usually occur where water fluoride levels are above the recommend levels of 0.7 to 1.2 parts per million and in general is quite rare.

*Natural water contains several different, and to us invisible, elements
in minute quantities that can be very useful to most diets.*

IODINE

Iodine is a chemical easily depleted from soil in limestone areas and bread or table salt is often fortified with iodide or iodate. In the body 60 percent is stored within the thyroid.

Chemical symbol: I.

RDA: 100–300µg needed daily. EC RDA: 150µg; USA RDA: 150µg; UK RNI: 140µg. Maximum safe level for self supplementation 500µg.

Best natural source: Kelp, iodized salt, fortified bread, fish, vegetables, onions, cereals, meat.

Essential for: Iodine is essential for hormones that work to control metabolic chemistry within the body. The thyroid hormones tri-iodothyronine and thyroxine are crucial to growth and development. Iodine can help with fat metabolism and mental acuity as well as having a beneficial effect on the appearance of hair, nails, and skin.

For such strange looking and diverse group of plants, kelp is remarkable useful to us.

Uses: It is sometimes given to people who may have been contaminated with radioactive iodine to reduce the absorption of the radioactive form. Radioactive iodine is sometimes used medicinally to reduce the activity of the thyroid gland (by permanently damaging it). This happens in cases of thyrotoxicosis which results in overactivity of the thyroid.

Iodine compounds have been used in some x-ray procedures, as well as in some cough remedies. It was previously used as an antiseptic in many households but is rarely found in pharmacies nowadays.

A deliciously healthy meal brimming with micronutrients. White fish supply a good portion of iodine, selenium, potassium, and phosphorus.

Supplements: Supplements should be avoided in pregnancy or if taking thyroxine supplements. They can be found in doses of 0.15µg or in multimineral preparations.

Iodine is most commonly taken in the form of kelp supplements. Kelp, a generic name for many seaweed species, provides many other minerals in small amounts but it is exceptional in its iodine levels. Typical supplements may also include calcium, and provide an iodine dose of 140µg. Recommended to take three tablets daily.

Deficiency: Shortage of iodine can lead to the formation of a goiter, a lump on the neck which is in fact a swelling of the thyroid gland. Alternatively it can lead to hyperthyroidism which leads to an underactive thyroid. Iodine deficiency in newborn babies can lead to cretinism. Cretinism is a condition characterized by stunted growth, specific facial features, and mental handicap. A complete cure is possible with thyroxine therapy if the condition is recognized early enough.

93

Excess: If incorrectly taken, prescribed iodine can be harmful. When
taken after a long period of time on a low iodine diet, supplements
can cause thyrotoxicosis. Rarely they can cause allergic reactions
with symptoms that include rash, abdominal pain, vomiting,
headaches, and facial swelling.

SPIRULINA AND CHLORELLA

Spirulina and chlorella are microalgae that have similar nutrient
profiles to kelp. Popular with vegans and vegetarians, supplements of
these plants may not actually be really useful unless taken in large
quantities. Typical supplement of 3mg can supply beta carotene, iron,
selenium, and B12 in reasonable levels, but taking them as food
provides a much wider range of useful micronutrients. In addition,
spirulina is a good source of the essential fatty acid GLA. Both plants
contain high levels of chlorophyll, a green pigment that reputedly
helps remove heavy metals from the body and reduces the effects of
radiation.

IRON

A metallic trace element, needed in tiny dietary amounts. Most men
have about 1–4g in their bodies and women have about half this
amount, although some may have no stores at all. It is found in the
complex compounds hemoglobin, myoglobin, and some cell enzymes. It
is stored in the liver, spleen, and bone marrow.

Uptake of iron is influenced by the type of iron ingested.
Only about eight percent of the total ingested is absorbed. The organically bound kind (from animal sources) is easily absorbed, but the
inorganic form (found in vegetables) is less readily absorbed.

Interestingly, vegetable-sourced iron is better absorbed with vitamin C. Other factors essential for the uptake and assimilation of iron include copper, cobalt, manganese, and vitamin C.

A couple of things can affect your uptake: tannic acids found in tea react with inorganic iron reducing its absorption (if excessive amounts are drunk), while phosphoric acid found in fizzy drinks and phytic acid from wheat bran may also have the same effect.

Known as an anticancer food, broccoli is rich in many minerals, as well as folates and phytochemicals.

Chemical symbol: Fe.
RDA: EC RDA: 14mg; USA RDA: 18mg; UK RNI men: 8.7mg; women: 14.8mg.
Maximum safe level for self supplementation 15mg.
Best natural source: Found in a variety of foods; liver, offal, meat, eggs, whole grain cereals, fish, green leafy vegetables, broccoli, potatoes, nuts, and soya beans.

From the same plant family as garlic, onions are a very useful food to have in your diet, providing some medicinal benefits along with their nutritional value.

Essential for: The formation and action of some enzymes, hemoglobin (essential red, oxygen carrying pigment in the blood) and myoglobin (red pigment in the muscles). Needed for metabolism of B vitamins.

Uses: Given to pregnant women.

Supplements: Sometimes listed as a ferrous compound i.e. ferrous sulfate. Organic compounds (gluconates, fumarates, or chelated to an amino acid) are better tolerated and do not neutralize vitamin E. Some people can be sensitive to the iron compounds in multivitamins (common symptoms are nausea or constipation).

Iron can be bought as a liquid supplement in a tonic. This is useful to those who can't swallow pills or capsules. The instructions should be followed carefully to avoid overdosing. People who drink a large quantities of tea and coffee can inhibit iron absorption.

For most people, teenagers, vegetarians, menstruating women, convalescents, and the elderly, a general multivitamin compound containing iron should act as sufficient health insurance. If you think you are anemic you should see your doctor.

Iron supplements should be kept well away from children: most cases of toxicity relate to accidental overdose in young children.

Deficiency: Iron is regularly lost in minute amounts through minor bleeding, when dead cells peel off the skin, and from dead cells of the lining of the bowel that are found in feces. Symptoms of deficiency can include abdominal pain, black feces, (signs of peptic ulcer), brittle nails, sore mouth or tongue in conjunction with fatigue or a headache.

Deficiency can arise from a diet low in iron, or a malabsorption disorder. Iron deficiency anemia is usually caused by abnormal blood loss, and insufficient intake to replenish the iron lost. It can arise from heavy periods (in women); diseases that are responsible for persistent bleeding in the digestive tract, such as gastritis, peptic

*A cheap source of vitamin C, potatoes are a food staple to many
diets providing many minerals and a lot of fiber too.*

ulcers, stomach cancer, or inflammatory bowel disease, hemor-rhoids; in some countries hookworm infestation can be the cause. Vegetarians are at risk from low iron intake as an unsupplemented diet provides mostly inorganic, poorly-absorbed sources of this mineral.

Women who begin pregnancy with little or no stores of iron are often prescribed supplements. During pregnancy the mother experiences an increased iron demand to meet the needs of the growing baby as it establishes its own blood supply.

Excess: Can cause nausea, diarrhea, constipation, or abdominal pain; the feces may turn black. Excessive intake over a long time may cause cirrhosis of the liver.

MAGNESIUM

Metallic element of which we have about 35g in the body, mostly dis-tributed in bones and teeth as a compound. Its functions are closely tied to those of calcium. Because of its connections to the nervous system, it is sometimes called the anti-stress mineral. Diuretics and alcohol deplete levels: the body finds it one of the hardest minerals to absorb.

Chemical symbol: Mg.

RDA: EC RDA: 300mg; USA RDA: 400mg; UK RNI men:
300mg; women: 270mg.
Maximum safe level for self supplementation 350mg.

Best natural source: Whole grain cereals, soya beans, nuts (brazils in particular), milk, fish, meat, raisins, dried figs, dried apricots, pota-toes, peas, lemons, grapefruit.

Essential for: The structure of bones and teeth, for the transmission of nerve impulses, muscle contraction, and enzyme formation.

With calcium and phosphorus it is essential for optimum skeletal strength and structure. In conjunction with vitamin B6 it ensures calcium is deposited in the bones. Pregnant and breast feeding women require higher levels than average intakes normally supply.

Uses: Tests show levels of magnesium in the blood may drop before menstruation. It also has a role in regulating blood sugar levels. Supplements are sometimes used to help stave off sugar cravings and premenstrual cramps.

Because it plays a vital role in muscle contraction, it is sometimes given as an injection of magnesium sulfate to heart attack patients in hospital. It may also be useful in preventing heart disease.

Research is still ongoing about its role in helping myalgic encephalopathy (ME; post-viral flu) sufferers with muscle pain and increasing energy levels.

Brazil nuts have exceptionally high levels of both magnesium and selenium.

Supplements: Usual doses available are 50–200mg. Ingredients may be listed as magnesium carbonate or magnesium oxide—both inorganic sources that are not as readily absorbed as the organic compounds. Frequently found in bone or premenstrual targeted formulations. Supplements should not be taken after meals as it neutralizes stomach acidity, and will therefore slow down the digestive processes.

Deficiency: Can occur as a result of severe kidney disease, alcohol dependence, malabsorption disorders, or prolonged treatment with diuretic or digitalis drugs.

Symptoms are anxiety, restlessness, tremors, palpitations, and depression. It may also lead to an increased risk of kidney stones or coronary artery disease.

Excess: Can occur after taking too much antacid or laxatives containing magnesium compounds. May show as nausea, vomiting, diarrhea, dizziness, and muscle weakness. Mild excess does not require treatment; severe excess can lead to heart damage or respiratory failure. In cases of an overdose, hospitalization is an absolute requirement in order that breathing and heart activity can be closely monitored and any action taken as necessary.

BORON

It's only since the 1980s that boron has been found to be an important trace element. Research has shown that it can slow down both calcium and magnesium loss from bones during and after the menopause and that it may have a beneficial effect on arthritis sufferers. It can be found in bone and menopause supplements; maximum daily dose should not excess 3mg. In foods it can be found in nuts and dried fruit, vegetables, and soya.

MANGANESE

Large intakes of calcium and phosphorus will impair absorption of manganese; those who eat a lot of meat and drink a lot of milk should increase the amount they intake. People who are absent minded might benefit from adding more to their diet.

Chemical symbol: Mn.

RDA: EC RDA: 2mg; USA RDA: 2mg; UK RNI men: 1.4mg; women: 1.2mg.

   Maximum safe level for self supplementation 15mg.

Best natural source: Nuts, peas, leafy green vegetables, egg yolks, whole grain cereals.

Essential for: Needed for the work of some enzymes, and involved with proper use of thiamine (B1) biotin, and vitamin C. Important to the formation of thyroxine (a thyroid hormone), proper digestion, normal bone structure, reproduction, and maintenance of the central nervous system.

Uses: It is used to help improve memory, prevent fatigue, and reduce nervous irritability.

Supplements: Found in multivitamin or mineral preparations in doses of 1–9mg.

Deficiency: Can cause ataxia—clumsiness and loss coordination— which affects limb or eye movements and balance.

Excess: Rare.

Peas are a great source of manganese.

Whole grain breads will provide a good source of complex carbohydrate (fiber) along with many vitamins and minerals.

MOLYBDENUM

A trace element needed in very small amounts for optimum health.

Chemical symbol: Mb.
RDA: None established but daily intake of 45–500µg is adequate.
Best natural source: Whole grains, legumes, dark green leafy vegetables.

Above: Butter beans are full of minerals and with a low glycaemic index too.

Essential for: Needed for proper utilization of iron (as it forms part of essential enzyme in the conversion of iron to hemoglobin), aids carbohydrate and fat metabolism.
Supplements: Not available. Adequate can be garnered from natural food sources.
Deficiency: None known.
Excess: Rare although 5–10 parts per million is considered toxic.

PHOSPHORUS

The salts of phosphorus, phosphates, are an essential part of the diet. About 85 percent of the body's phosphate is combined with calcium

Leafy green vegetables like Chinese leaves provide many of the essential minerals as well as a few trace elements.

103

Duck without its skin (like many other meats) isn't as fatty as many think. Combined with a delicious raspberry sauce, as it is here, it's a good source of B vitamins, selenium, iron, zinc, and phosphorus.

in the bones and teeth while the rest is distributed through most tissues. Too much iron, aluminum, and manganese can render it ineffective.

Chemical symbol: P.

RDA: EC RDA: 800mg; USA RDA: 1000mg; UK RNI men: 550mg.

Maximum safe level for self supplementation 1500mg.

Best natural source: Cereals, eggs, meat, dairy produce, fish, nuts, seeds.

Essential for: It helps to maintain the acid-alkali balance of many body fluids including the blood, urine, and saliva. Importantly it is also part of the compound ATP (adenosine triphopshate) which provides the energy for chemical reactions in the cells. Vitamin D and calcium are essential to its proper functioning; niacin (vitamin B3) cannot be digested without phosphorus. Also required for normal kidney function, transfer of nerve impulses, and heart regularity.

Supplements: Found in many multivitamin or multimineral preparations.

Deficiency: The kidneys are the organs that maintain the level of phosphates in the body so the body compensates for a slight deficiency of phosphates by excreting less in the urine. Hypophosphatemia (low levels of phosphate) can occur to sufferers of hyperparathyroidism; after long-term treatment with diuretic drugs; as a result of malabsorption disorders; or prolonged starvation. Symptoms are bone pain, weakness, seizures, and, in severe cases, coma then death.

Excess: Diarrhea is a side effect of taking phosphate drugs to correct hyperphosphatemia. In middle age our ability to excrete excess phosphorus is reduced.

POTASSIUM

An average-sized person has about 140g of potassium, distributed through the cells. Most food contains potassium and deficiency is rare. Alcohol, coffee, sugar, and diuretics have a negative effect on potassium.

Chemical symbol: K.

RDA: EC RDA: 3500mg;
USA RDA:
3500mg; UK
RNI: 3500mg.

Best natural
source:
Lean meat,
whole grains,
green leafy
vegetables,
bananas, oranges,
beans, watercress, mint
leaves, sunflower seeds.

Essential for: In conjunction
with sodium and calcium,

Bananas are famous for their potassium content, as well as being delicious.

Fennel, a rich source of potassium, is delicious roasted with other winter vegetables, although some find the mild aniseed flavor off-putting.

potassium helps maintain a normal heart rhythm, regulates the body's water balance, conducts nerve impulses and is responsible for the contraction of muscles.

Supplements: Available as separate high dose up to 600mg as potassium gluconate. Also found in many multivitamin or multimineral formulations.

Deficiency: Low levels are rarely due to insufficient intake through diet. It may occur as the result of a digestive disorder such as gastroenteritis. Children are especially vulnerable to this type of loss. Other reasons why a deficiency might occur include prolonged use of diuretic drugs, use of corticosteroids, overuse of laxatives, diabetes, or Cushing's syndrome, certain kidney disease, and excessive coffee or alcohol intake.

106

Hypoglycemia (low blood sugar) or a long fast can also cause
low levels of potassium as can mental or physical stress. People on
low carbohydrate diets may have reduced levels.

Symptoms of mild deficiency are fatigue, dizziness, drowsiness,
and muscle weakness.

Excess: Not common, but may be caused by excess supplements to
correct a deficiency, severe
kidney failure, or Addision's
disease. Result in tingling and
numbness, muscle paralysis,
heart rhythm disturbance.

SELENIUM

An essential trace element. Half of the body's supplies of 5–10mg are found in the liver. It works
synergistically with vitamin E; both are
potent antioxidants.

Levels found in vegetables
are definitely subject to soil quality. Finland
has very low levels and adds selenium to
fertilizers and animal feed; Britain also has
low levels.

*Fresh trout are full of good
things, vitamins B1, B2, B3, B6,
B12, D, E, and B5 along with
potassium, phosphorus, iodine, and
selenium.*

Chemical symbol: Se.

RDA: EC RDA: none; USA RDA: none; UK RNI men: 75µg; women: 60µg.
Maximum safe level for self supplementation 200µg.

Best natural source: Whole grains, dairy produce, meat, fish, onions, broccoli.

Essential for: Many of its functions are linked with vitamin E. Together they help maintain the immune system. Selenium is part of a key antioxidant enzyme, gluthianone peroxidase, which protects the fatty parts of cells. Required for the production of thyroxine, a thyroid hormone which helps regulate metabolic rate. Males have a greater need for it; their supplies are concentrated in the testes and seminal ducts—selenium is lost in semen.

Uses: Selenium sulfide is a constituent of some dandruff shampoos. Selenium helps the body to produce anti-inflammatory prostaglandins, which may help alleviate some of the symptoms of rheumatoid arthritis. It can apparently alleviate hot flushes and the distress of menopause.

Versatile vegetables, onions, form the basis of many stews and stirfrys which means it is hard not to reap their nutritional benefits.

Supplements: Supplements can be found in 100 or 200µg strengths, often with vitamins C, E, and zinc. Multivitamin preparations include small amounts which will augment any deficiency in the diet. For therapeutic effects higher doses are required. Organic selenium is normally the best absorbed form; frequently it is found in yeast preparations or as seleno-methionine.

Deficiency: No known effect. Low levels are linked to increased risk of cancer and heart disease—and cancer sufferers often have levels 30 percent lower than non-cancer sufferers. Vegetarians, excessive junk food eaters, the elderly, smokers, and pregnant or breast feeding women may be at risk from low levels.

Excess: High selenium intake may cause breath and urine to smell of garlic. Some selenium compounds may cause skin irritation or if inhaled can irritate the respiratory tract. Supplement intakes of 1mg for a period of two years can cause nausea, in addition to hair and nail changes.

SODIUM

The average person has 55g of sodium distributed through the body; the levels in the blood are controlled by the kidneys which eliminate an excess in the urine. High intakes will result in depletion of potassium.

Chemical symbol: Na.

RDA: There is no official RDA although suggested intake is 1–3g.

Best natural source: Most foods contain sodium and it is frequently added in the cooking process as salt or sodium bicarbonate. Main sources are salt, processed foods, cheese, bread, cereals, smoked, pickled, or cured meat and fish. Pickles and snack foods contain large amounts.

Essential for: Needed to help maintain the body's water balance, normal heart rhythm, and is involved in the conduction of impulses along the nerves.

Uses: In hot climates sodium supplements or salt tablets (in

Cured meats are a good source of salt and sodium. A craving for bacon may arise out of a need for more fat in the diet.

addition to water) may prevent heat disorders by replacing sodium lost through sweating.

Supplements: Rarely needed. Kelp is a good source.

Deficiency: Rare. Symptoms include tiredness, weakness, muscle
cramps, and dizziness. In extreme cases there may be a drop in
blood pressure leading to confusion, fainting, and palpitations.
Treatment is to take supplements. Deficiency usually occurs after
loss through unshakable diarrhea or vomiting, copious sweating,
or long-term treatment with anti-diuretic drugs. In some cases it
can be caused by cystic fibrosis, kidney disorders, or underactive
adrenal glands. Deficiency can result in less efficient carbohydrate
digestion.

Excess: Most western diets contain far too much salt. High intake is
thought to contribute to hypertension (high blood pressure).
People with high blood pressure who also ingest high levels of
sodium could increase their risk of heart disease, kidney damage,
or stroke. Other side effects include fluid retention, which in
extreme cases, may cause dizziness and swollen legs. Intakes of
over 14g of sodium chloride (chemical name for salt) are toxic.

SULFUR

**If you are getting enough protein in your diet, you will also be acquir-
ing adequate supplies of sulfur.**

Chemical symbol: S.

RDA: None established.

Best natural source: Lean beef, dried beans, eggs, fish, cabbage.

Essential for: Sulfur is a constituent of vitamin B1 (thiamine) and
several amino acids. It is needed to manufacture collagen, which is

important to bones, tendons, and connective tissues. It is also a constituent of keratin, the main component of hair, nails, and skin. It helps maintain oxygen balance for proper brain function.

Uses: It is used in some creams and ointments to treat a variety of skin disorders including acne, dandruff, psoriasis, scabies, nappy rash, and some fungal infections.

Supplements: Dietary supplements are not commonly available.

Deficiency: Not known.

Excess: Large amounts of inorganic sulfur are toxic.

Have you ever smelt a rotten egg? The compound responsible is found in eggs and is called iron sulphide, a potent and once smelt never forgotten aroma!

VANADIUM

Trace element that doesn't need to be supplemented in the diet: dine on fish regularly and get your full requirement. Chemical symbol is V. There is no RDA for this mineral. The best natural sources are found in fish. It's essential for the inhibition cholesterol formation in the blood vessels. Its synthetic form is toxic in excess but there are not records of a deficiency problem. Supplements are not available.

ZINC

A vital mineral for well-being, zinc has been identified as being involved in over 80 body processes. Many women between 16 and 24 do not manage to get enough in their diet. Zinc is lost in food processing.

Chemical symbol: Zn.

RDA: EC RDA: 15mg; USA RDA: 15mg; UK RNI men: 9.5mg;
    women: 7mg.
        Maximum safe level for self supplementation 15mg.

Best natural source: Small amounts are present in many foods. Lean
    meat, wholemeal bread, whole grain cereals, dried beans, seafood,
    ground mustard, pumpkin seeds, wheat germ, eggs.

Essential for: Normal growth and development of reproductive organs, prostate gland, healing of wounds, manufacture of proteins and nucleic acids, metabolism of fatty acids. It also controls the activities of many enzymes and is involved in the function of insulin. It is also an antioxidant mineral that is very useful for immune system functioning. It helps maintain the balance of the acid-alkali balance in the blood.

It's been known for sometime that oysters are good for you, and it's the zinc that gives them their boost.

Uses: Zinc preparations are used to treat skin and scalp disorders.

It is also found in nappy rash creams (and rust-proofing paints).

It has also been identified as a factor in anorexia nervosa— a zinc deficiency contributes to the lack of desire to eat by diminishing the senses of taste and smell—and it can therefore be used as part of the treatment.

Anecdotal evidence suggests that zinc may be helpful in improving benign enlargement of the prostate gland.

Zinc is good for the immune system, and pecans, a potent source, are a tasty way of keeping it in optimum condition.

Supplements: A common ingredient of multivitamin and multimineral preparations, although the dose varies from 1–15mg. For health insurance top-up doses of 5–10mg are sufficient, whereas for cold prevention or skin conditions a higher dose is suggested. As with other minerals, the inorganic compounds may not be as well absorbed as the organic ones: zinc chelated with amino acids is very well absorbed.

Cold lozenges sometimes contain zinc in levels 3–7mg per lozenge.

Copper levels can be depleted by prolonged zinc intake, so it may be useful to have both in a supplement.

Deficiency: Rare. Occurs in people who are malnourished or those with a malabsorption disorder, or a disorder of zinc absorption.

Deficiency can happen when there is increased requirement by the cells to cope with damage such as sickle cell anemia or after burns. Symptoms include loss of appetite and damage to taste and smell perception. Hair loss and inflammation of skin, mouth, tongue, and eyelids are other recognizable symptoms.

In children, deficiency impairs growth and delays sexual development. In men, low levels may reduce sperm counts and women with low zinc levels may give birth to lower weight babies.

Mild deficiency can lead to delayed wound healing; reduce appetite, poor skin condition, and white flecks on the nails.

Excess: Excess and prolonged intake generally happens after over-supplementation. Intakes over 30mg can interfere with absorption of minerals iron and copper (and can lead to a deficiency in them), and excess may also affect folic acid levels. Symptoms include nausea, vomiting, fever, headaches, tiredness, and abdominal pain.

WATER

Water is essential to all forms of life and is the most common chemical in the body. It makes up to three quarters of body weight, with two thirds being distributed in the cells and the rest is extracellular in the blood plasma, lymph, cerebrospinal fluid, and tissue fluid.

Chemical symbol: H_2O.

RDA: No specific RDA but it is recommended that we should aim to drink six to eight glasses daily or 84.5 US fl.oz/88 UKfl.oz. (2.5 liters).

Essential for: Necessary solvent for digestion and all body reactions; it provides the medium for the transportation of most substances in the body. The blood plasma carries water to all cells and

*If you are physically active or have a high salt
diet, your need for water might increase.*

eliminates excess water from liver, lungs, skin, and delivers to the kidneys where it is filtered prior to excretion.

The balance of water is maintained within very narrow limits. The activities of the kidneys control intake and output with the help of hormones. The minimum amount required to flush out metabolic waste products is 0.5 liters; most healthy adults produce 1.5 liters of urine a day.

If there is an excessive amount of a substance dissolved in the blood that needs to be excreted, more water is required. This is usually compensated for by an increased water intake in response to thirst, but it can lead to dehydration.

Deficiency: Dehydration. People with fevers should drink frequently to help flush out toxins and waste products and in order to prevent dehydration.

Excess: Can result in edema (the accumulation of water in the body tissues) as the result of disorders such as kidney failure or heart failure, and insufficient urine is excreted. Excess intake (16 to 24 glasses in an hour) can be dangerous for an adult.

Chemicals in Water: Tap water is frequently treated in some way with chemicals to purify it. Chlorine is the main additive although fluoride is also added in some areas. Chlorinated water destroys vitamin E and those who drink it should also eat bio yogurt to replace intestinal bacteria destroyed by it. Alternatively, filter water before drinking it to remove unwanted chemicals and improve the taste. Water softeners add sodium and "soften" hard water. Hard water contains lots of calcium and magnesium.

TISSUE SALTS

Tissue salts (sometimes also called cell salts) are a collection of inorganic compounds that are used in homeopathic medicine. They are also known as Schuessler salts after the man that first described them, Dr. Wilhelm Heinrich Schuessler, at the end of the 19th century. He was a German doctor who also studied biochemistry, physics, and homoeopathy: the formulation of the "Biochemic System of Medicine" is attributed to him. He isolated the salts below—their names are reminiscent of early compound names which have now been standardized.

Dr. Schuessler believed that a deficiency in any of the tissue salts weakens cell structure and could cause illness; if the deficiency was rectified, the body restores a balanced cell structure and so heals itself. This biochemic system of medicine apparently works best after detailed diagnosis of facial signs that evidently show long before any physical symptoms are revealed. Once a diagnosis has been made the appropriate salts can be supplemented.

Homeopathy is based on symptomatology and the laws of similars: "let likes be treated by likes." Very small amounts of a substance are used to treat the symptoms produced by the same substance in a huge dose. Whenever anyone is thinking of taking homeopathic remedies, it's a good idea to consult a qualified person in order to gain the full benefit of the homeopath's knowledge and skills. Many people are skeptical about homeopathy, but those in favor shouldn't approach it blindly. Tissue salts are safe except if you are lactose intolerant.

THE 12 TISSUE SALTS AND THEIR FUNCTIONS:

• Fluoride of lime, calcium phosphoricum, phosophate of lime [calcium fluoride]
Part of the connective tissues of the body that maintain the elasticity of

tissues. Imbalance can cause poor circulation, varicose veins, late dentition, muscle tendon strain, carbuncles, and cracked skin. Chiefly used for conditions originating in muscular or supportive tissues and for treating rapidly decaying teeth.

• **Phosphate of lime [calcium phosphate]**
Calcium phosphate is found in bones and teeth. It is the most abundant tissue salt in the body. An imbalance can be the cause of numbness, cold hands and feet, sore breasts, and night sweats. This tissue salt can help to speed up convalescence and is indicated for blood and bone disorders including osteoporosis and anemia.

• **Sulfate of lime, calcarea sulphorica, gypsum [calcium sulfate]**
A component of all connective tissues as well as important to the liver. An imbalance can be the cause of conditions associated with the discharge of pus: skin eruptions, deep abscesses, and ulcers. It helps to remove waste products from the blood stream. If taken at the first sign of a sore throat or cold it can be very effective.

• **Ferrum phosphate [iron phosphate]**
Part of the blood and all other cells, except nerve cells. It is useful in treating inflammatory conditions such as colds, infections, pain, and fever as well as nosebleeds and excessive menses. It is useful in the treatment of stuffy noses, and sore throats and in general first aid.

• **Chloride of potash, Kalium muriaticum [potassium chloride/ carbonate]**
An imbalance of this tissue salt can cause granulation of the eyelids, blistering eczema, and warts. Deficiency in this salt is also implicated in allergies, sinusitis, snoring, and nausea. It is used as the main remedy for catarrhal conditions.

While we may not realize it, our body language and manner
reveal a lot to others about our state of mind. If you are feeling the
pressure, take stock of your diet: you can boost your morale
and your appearance with the right foods.

- **Kalium phosphate [potassium phosphate]**

Found in all body tissues but concentrated in brain, nerve, and blood cells. An imbalance can cause incomplete fat digestion, poor memory, and a faint rapid pulse. It is used to treat a lack of concentration, grumpiness, insomnia, physical and mental fatigue, and some nervous conditions.

- **Sulfate of potash, kalium sulfate, kali sulphuricum [potassium sulfate]**

This tissue salt interacts with the internal organ linings and skin cells. A deficiency could cause skin eruptions, feelings of heaviness and pains in the limbs. It is important for healthy skin, hair, and mucous membranes. It is used when there is sticky, yellow discharge from the skin or mucous membranes.

- **Phosphate of magnesium [magnesium phosphate]**

A mineral component of teeth, bones, nerves, muscles, brain, and blood cells. A deficiency can cause flatulence, hunger pains, nervous tension, muscle cramps. It is quick to relieve pain so is used in the treatment of menstrual pains, neuralgia, shooting pains, and colic.

- **Natrium muriaticum, chloride of soda [sodium chloride]**

As you might expect this is the water balancing tissue salt. An imbalance or deficiency can cause salt cravings, hayfever, and watery discharges from the eyes and nose, dry lips, lack of vitality, and itchy skin.

- **Natrium phosphate [sodium phosphate]**

In the body this tissue salt emulsifies fatty acid and ensures uric acid remains soluble in the blood. (Uric acid is a waste product that we excrete as urine.) An imbalance can cause sour breath, jaundice, and an acid or coppery taste in the mouth. It is indicated for treatment of heartburn, acid indigestion, cholesterol problems, smelly feet and body odor, and sleeplessness due to poor digestion.

• Natrium sulfate, natrium sulphuricum [sodium sulfate]

A stimulant for natural secretions but it is a slight irritant to tissues. It promotes the elimination of excess water from the body. It is used for the healthy functioning of the liver and is recommended for disorders to do with the liver (alcoholism, jaundice, and hepatitis.) An imbalance can be the cause of fevers, edema, depression, and gallbladder problems.

• Silicea, silicic acid

A component of all connective tissues as well as those of the hair, skin, and nails. A deficiency can cause poor memory, carbuncles, hair problems, and ribbed or ingrowing nails. It is an important anti-stress tissue salt, used to treat irritability, noise or light sensitivity, intense headaches, and involuntary twitching of facial muscles. It has a reputation for being able to remove foreign matter from the body so should therefore not be used for long periods by people with implants or other objects in their body. Eating whole grain foods should supply an adequate supply of this salt.

In addition to the properties listed above, Schuessler recommended the five phosphates for functional nervous disturbances and for brain fatigue due to overwork and worry. A balanced combination of all 12 remedies reputedly gives protections against deficiencies.

Whole grain foods are staple foods to many people, supplying a wide range of nutrients.

HELP YOURSELF

The following is a quick guide that may help you to see if you have a possible vitamin deficiency. If you feel you have serious symptoms and feel unwell then you should always consult a medical practitioner for advice.

Arthritis
Avoid: anchovies, asparagus, veined cheese, red wine.
Vitamins: C, D, E.
Avocado, butter, cabbage, citrus fruits, egg yolk, green bell peppers, liver, nuts, potatoes, tomatoes, vegetables oils, fish oils such as mackerel, salmon, or sardines.

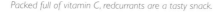

Halitosis
Vitamins: Niacin (B3), C.
Cabbage, citrus fruits, fish, green bell pepper, legumes, liver, meat, potatoes, tomatoes, and whole grains.
Minerals: Zinc.
Pumpkin seeds, shellfish, sunflower seeds, vegetables, wheat germ, whole grains.

Cholesterol
Vitamins: B complex and inositol.
Brewer's yeast, cantaloupe, dried beans, raisins, yeast.

Packed full of vitamin C, redcurrants are a tasty snack.

MUSCLES

Cramp
Vitamins: Thiamine (B1), B6, biotin, D.
Brewer's yeast, butter, egg yolk, fish, fish liver oils, legumes, liver, meat, organ meats, nuts, potatoes, pork, whole grain cereals.
Minerals: Calcium, chlorine, magnesium, sodium.
Beans, cereals and grains, dairy products, fruit, leafy green vegetables, meat, nuts, olives, seafood, salt, sardines.

Bell peppers are bursting with bioflavonoids, useful insurance against bruising.

INTESTINE AND BOWEL PROBLEMS

Constipation
Vitamins: B complex.
Cheese, beef, liver, kidney, pork.

Gastric
Vitamins: Thiamine (B1), riboflavin (B2) B5 pantothenic acid, C, choline, folic acid/PABA.
Beef, brewer's yeast, eggs, cheese, fish, fresh leafy green vegetables, fruit, green bell pepper, legumes, milk, liver, kelp, kidney, nuts, olives, potatoes, pork, rye flour, tomatoes, whole grains, yeast.

Limes are a good cure for many illnesses from arthritis to diarrhea.

Diarrhea

Vitamins: Riboflavin (B2), niacin (B3), C, K.

Alfalfa, avocado, brewer's yeast, cabbage, cheese, citrus, eggs, fruits, fish, fish liver oils, green bell pepper, kidney, kelp, legumes, lean meat, liver, milk, pepper, potatoes, poultry, tomatoes, yeast, yogurt.

Minerals: Zinc.

Pumpkin seeds, shellfish, sunflower seeds, vegetables, wheat germ, whole grains.

Unsaturated fatty acids:

Peanuts, sunflower seeds, vegetable oils, walnuts.

HEAD AND MIND

Dizziness
Minerals: Manganese.
Milk, leafy green vegetables, liver, kidney, yeast.

Forgetfulness/bad memory
Vitamins: Thiamine (B1).
Brewer's yeast, legumes, liver, nuts, potatoes, pork, whole grains.
Minerals: Manganese.
Egg yolks, leafy green vegetables, nuts, peas, whole grain cereals.

Tomatoes are a useful source of vitamins C, E, and beta carotene.

Dandruff
Vitamins: B12, B6.
Beef, eggs, fish, kidney, legumes, liver, whole grain cereals, yeast.
Minerals: Selenium.
Bran, broccoli, tomatoes, tuna, onions, wheat germ.
Unsaturated fatty acids:
Peanuts, sunflower seeds, vegetable oils, walnuts.

Graying hair
Vitamins B complex.
Liver, pork, kidney, cheese, beef.
Minerals: Iodine.
Dairy foods, seafood, iodized salt, kelp.
Unsaturated fatty acids:
Peanuts, sunflower seeds, vegetable oils, walnuts.

125

Pineapples are the main source of a photochemical bromelian which has been shown to ease arthritis and improve digestion.

Hair loss
Vitamins: Biotin, inositol, B complex, C, folic acid.
Beef, brewer's yeast, cabbage, cheese, citrus fruits, fresh leafy green vegetables, green bell pepper, kidney, lecithin, liver, nuts, pork, potatoes, tomatoes, whole grains.

Worry
Vitamins: B6, B12, niacin B3, PABA.
Beef, brewer's yeast, cantaloupe, dried lima beans, eggs, fish, legumes, meat, organ meats, whole grain cereals, yeast, raisins.
Minerals: Magnesium.
Cereals and grains, leafy green vegetables, seafoods.

EYE PROBLEMS

Visual acuity focusing
Vitamins: B2.
Butter, cream, egg yolks, fish, leafy green or yellow vegetables, liver.

Night blindness
Vitamins: A.
Eggs, cheese, fish, milk, liver, kidney, yeast.

GENERAL HEALTH

Fatigue
Vitamins: A, B complex, C, D.
Beef, butter, cabbage, cheese, citrus fruits, cream, egg yolks, fish, fish liver oils, green bell pepper, leafy green or yellow vegetables, liver, kidney, pork, potatoes, tomatoes.

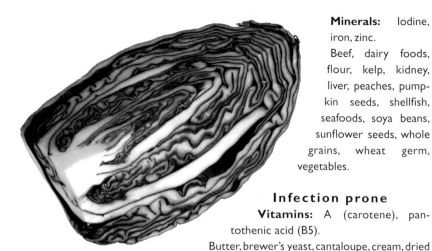

Minerals: Iodine, iron, zinc.

Beef, dairy foods, flour, kelp, kidney, liver, peaches, pumpkin seeds, shellfish, seafoods, soya beans, sunflower seeds, whole grains, wheat germ, vegetables.

Infection prone

Vitamins: A (carotene), pantothenic acid (B5).

Butter, brewer's yeast, cantaloupe, cream, dried lima beans, fish, egg yolks, leafy green or yellow vegetables, liver, raisins.

Thought to contain natural antiseptic properties, red cabbage may be useful in fighting skin infections.

Sleeplessness

Vitamins: B complex, biotin.

Beef, cheese, kidney, liver, pork, brewer's yeast, kidney, liver, nuts.

Minerals: Calcium, potassium.

Bananas, beans, citrus fruits, cereals, dairy products, meat, leafy green vegetables, sunflower seeds, watercress.

Mouth sores

Vitamins: Riboflavin (B2), B6.

Eggs, cheese, fish, milk, legumes, meat, organ meats, whole grain cereals, yeast.

Nosebleed
Vitamins: C, K, bioflavonoids.
Alfalfa, cabbage, citrus fruits, fish liver oils, green pepper, potatoes, kelp tomatoes, yogurt.
Lemon, lime, orange, or tangerine peel.

Slow growth
Vitamins: Riboflavin (B2), folic acid.
Eggs, cheese, fish, fruit, milk, liver, leafy green vegetables, kidney, yeast.
Minerals: Zinc, cobalt.
Liver, kidney, pumpkin and sunflower seeds, shellfish, vegetables, wheat germ, whole grains.
Protein:
Dairy products, eggs, fish, meat, soya beans.

Slow healing
Vitamins: C, E, K.
Alfalfa, avocado, cabbage, citrus fruits, fish liver oils, green bell pepper, kelp, nuts, potatoes, tomatoes, yogurt, vegetables oils.
Minerals: Zinc.
Pumpkin seeds, shellfish, sunflower seeds, vegetables, wheat germ, whole grains.

Like apples in their nutrient profile, pears are packed with useful vitamins.

Red onions are useful in fighting off conditions such as dandruff.

Loss of appetite
Vitamins A, thiamine (B1), C, biotin.
Brewer's yeast, butter, cabbage, citrus fruits, cream, egg yolks, fish, green bell pepper, kidney, leafy green or yellow vegetables, legumes, liver, nuts, potatoes, pork, tomatoes, whole grains.
Minerals: Phosphorus, sodium, zinc.
Cheese, eggs, fish, legumes, meat, nuts, olives, poultry, pumpkin seeds, salt, sardines, shellfish, sunflower seeds, wheat germ, whole grains, vegetables.
Protein: Dairy products, eggs, fish, meat, soya beans.

Menstrual problems
Vitamins: B6, B12.
Beef, eggs, fish, legumes, meat, organ meats, whole grain cereals, yeast.

SKIN PROBLEMS

Eczema
Vitamins: A, B complex, inositol.
Brewer's yeast, butter, cantaloupe, cream, dried lima beans, egg yolks, fish, leafy green or yellow vegetables, liver, raisins.
Minerals Copper, iodine.
Dried legumes, organ meats, whole grain cereals, dairy foods, kelp, seafoods.

General dermatitis
Vitamins: Riboflavin (B2), B6, biotin, niacin (B3).
Brewer's yeast, eggs, cheese, fish, milk, legumes, meat, organ meats, nuts, whole grains, yeast.

Spots and acne

Vitamins A, B complex, C.

Beef, butter, cabbage, citrus fruits, cheese, cream, egg yolks, fish, green bell pepper, leafy green or yellow vegetables, kidney, liver, pork, potatoes, tomatoes.

Minerals: Zinc.

Pumpkin seeds, shellfish, sunflower seeds, vegetables, wheat germ, whole grains.

Alcohol related problems

Vitamins: B complex, A, D. Brewer's yeast, cantaloupe, dried beans, raisins, yeast, butter, cream, egg yolks, fish, leafy green or yellow vegetables, liver, butter, egg yolk, fish liver oils, liver, sunshine.

Minerals: Calcium, magnesium, phosphorus, zinc.

Beans, cheese, dairy products, eggs, fish, fruit, legumes, meat, poultry, nuts, leafy green vegetables, pumpkin seeds, seafoods, shellfish, sunflower seeds, whole grains, wheat germ, vegetables.

Grapes contain antioxidants which are known to reduce heart disease.

Right: A delicious way to destress, eat a few dried apricots and chill out.

3. ANTIOXIDANTS

WHAT ARE ANTIOXIDANTS?

Antioxidants are, literally, substances that prevent oxidation. Oxidation is a process that occurs when a substance reacts with oxygen to form a compound: rust is an easy example to see in everyday life. Exposed iron reacts with the oxygen in the air—particularly in the presence of water—to form iron oxide, a red compound that we call rust. In the body, at a molecular level, the oxidation process can be carcinogenic.

Antioxidants and their actions have been talked about quite a lot as something to look to include in our diets. If you eat a reasonably balanced diet, with lots of fruit, vegetables, and whole grain, you are probably already getting enough antioxidants, but did you know just how beneficial they can be? Antioxidants are supplied to the body in the form of vitamins, minerals, and phytochemicals from a balanced diet, and they help prevent oxidation by "mopping up" substances called oxygen free radicals.

Above: Oxidation in progress.

The main substances that are known to have an antioxidant effect are beta

Left: Fruits are a wonderful store of a range of useful substances—phytochemicals — that are still being investigated for their medicinal properties.

carotene (a precursor to vitamin A), vitamin C, vitamin E, the mineral selenium, and many phytochemicals—particularly carotenoids—have also been found to have antioxidant effects. Together, these substances are thought to be effective in helping to prevent cancer, heart disease, and stroke.

Why do we need antioxidants?

Oxidation is linked with the aging process—such as the formation of wrinkles and age spots—and with some diseases connected to aging like arthritis, cancer, and cataracts. It may seem strange that when every process in the body revolves around the acquisition and distribution of oxygen for cell respiration, we want to protect ourselves against the oxidation process. More specifically it is "free" radicals that we don't want to be present in large numbers.

Free radicals are a natural by product of the reactions of oxygen within cells in the energy releasing cycle.

They are all substances—molecules—that have unpaired electrons, and as such are unstable; in their attempt to become more stable they can do damage to cell walls, certain cell structures, and genetic material within the cells. (They are known to damage the structure of proteins, lipids, and nucleic acids.) In a person with a normal balanced diet, free radicals are held in check by antioxidant defense mechanisms. These mechanisms are part of the normal functioning of cell differentiation and growth, maintenance of the immune system, and DNA repair. It is an imbalance between the production and destruction of free radicals that is implicated in degenerative and aging processes. In the worst case, and over a long period of time, this damage can be irreversible and ultimately lead to disease (for example, cancer).

Oxygen free radicals, although they sound like the bad guys, are actually also very necessary in small numbers to help control excess harmful bacteria in the body. We know free radicals also play an important part in biological functions such as immunity, inflammation, growth, and repair, so they are important during infections. In excessive quantities, however, they do become more dangerous. In the body, excess intakes of polyunsaturated fat can promote their production. One of the things free radicals do though is turn cholesterol "sticky," so making it more likely that plaque will form and will block arteries. Stress is another

The best way to secure a full range of vitamins, minerals, and the protective effects of antioxidants is to eat five to seven portions of fresh fruit and vegetables daily.

factor in their production, as this increases the amount of the hormone adrenalin, which after use breaks down to form free radicals. Mostly, though, we are constantly fighting an onslaught of free radicals that arise from environmental sources, especially smoking, air pollution, x-rays, and sunlight (UV light). Organic chemicals (substances that contain the element carbon), as well as nitrogen oxide, and oxygen can be altered to be free radicals.

A diet high in fresh fruits and vegetables will be naturally high in antioxidants. Research seems to indicate it is better to acquire antioxidants as part of your diet than through supplements as they are more easily absorbed and therefore accessible to cell processes. There have been around 200 studies of the relationship between antioxidants present in fruit and vegetables and cancer. Overwhelmingly, the majority show that a high intake of antioxidant rich food has a protective effect.

Antioxidants factors:
• Beta carotene: found in brightly colored fruit and vegetables. It is particularly useful in protecting against the photo-aging of the skin exposed to UV rays in sunlight, but is not a substitute for sunscreen.
• Vitamin C: found in nuts, grains, seeds, and vegetables oils, especially wheat germ. Vitamin C protects the liquid internal parts of cells from free radicals. Its other antioxidant functions are thought to include helping to cut the risk of coronary heart disease; one trial has shown it to have an effect in dilating arteries and so improve blood flow.
• Vitamins E: citrus fruits, green bell peppers, blackcurrants, potatoes. In partnership with vitamin C, vitamin E protects the outer fatty part of cells from attack by free radicals. Together the two vitamins boost the body's natural defenses. Vitamins E's most

powerful antioxidant component is thought to be d-alpha tocopherol.

• Selenium: found in grains, fish, and meat. Selenium has been shown to protect against heart disease, some cancers, and premature aging. Selenium has a beneficial effect on people with rheumatoid arthritis and may reduce inflammation. It is toxic in excess; in the UK the precautionary maximum dosage for men is 450µg, and lower for women.

• Phytochemicals: bioflavonoids, carotenoids, glucosinolates, organosulfides, phytoestrogens.

Bell peppers are packed full of vitamin C and beta carotene, and the antioxidant action of vitamin C is thought to be helped by flavonoids.

PHYTOCHEMICALS

In addition to the wonderful array of vitamins and minerals that we get from fruit and vegetables in our diet, we are also getting a variety of substances that have been labeled phytochemicals (*phyto* means plant). It is estimated that there may be more than 100 different phytochemicals in just one serving of vegetables. These compounds have been described as "biologically active nutrients" and there are thousands of them.

Present in all plants to different degrees, they are the chemicals that confer color, flavor, and odor to each species. Due to the potential health benefits, much research has been carried out with respect to phytochemicals. It appears that they are protective, disease preventing compounds which have a role to play in the fight against cancer, heart disease, and other infections. Unsurprisingly many are also antioxidants while some have been found to block or suppress harmful cell reactions, but more is being discovered about them all the time. The following categories have been recognized so far.

Bioflavonoids

Also known as flavonoids, these compounds are occasionally classed together as vitamin P. They are water-soluble plant pigments that can be classified variously. One system divides them into the subgroups that are based on their chemical structure isoflavones, anthocyanins, flavans, flavonols, flavones, and flavanones. Their compounds are all based on two six-carbon rings joined by a three-carbon link, and are sometimes referred to as polyphenols.

Bioflavonoids are found in high quantities in plants that naturally have high levels of sugar, such as fruit and sweet vegetables; it is known that sugars aid their proper absorption when digested. They are responsible for the pigmentation in plants and they appear to be

essential for the proper function and absorption of vitamin C. One of the areas under research is the effect of bioflavonoids on the circulatory system, and they apparently strengthen the walls of capillaries thereby preventing bruising. Generally flavonoids been shown to have antiviral, antiallergic, anti-inflammatory, antithrombitic, and anticarcinogenic properties in the laboratory. As well as mopping up free radicals, flavonoids have an inhibitory action on prostaglandin synthesis and mediators of inflammation. They have also been shown to inhibit tyrosine kinases, which are involved in cell growth and development.

The flavones taxifolin and rutin are found in citrus fruits. Rutin and hesperidin along with catechins (found in green tea and which have been found to have antioxidant effects) may protect the circulatory system from damage.

Anthocyanins typically produce purple colors in plants and are found in wine and bilberry. One example, ellagic acid, is known to block the action of cancer-inducing cells and can be found in large quantities in strawberries, blackberries, cherries, and grapes.

Blackberries and cherries contain lots of ellagic acid.

Tea is a good antioxidant in moderate amounts, but should not be drunk with a meal as it can hinder absorption of some nutrients.

Anecdotal evidence from World War II recorded that British pilots had a habit of eating bilberry jam just prior to a night mission, and claimed that it radically improved their night vision. After the war, research was carried out into possible beneficial constituents. Bilberry is still recommended for a variety of eye disorders such as poor night vision and day blindness, and it is sometimes used in the hope of preventing macular degeneration, diabetic retinopathy, and cataracts.

The subgroup flavonols have been the most researched. Quercetin is an antioxidant found in black tea, red wine, onions, tomatoes, apples, potatoes, grapes, and broad beans. Studies have shown that (at high levels) it can lower the risk of coronary heart disease, and may also have a preventative action on cataract formation, as well as having antihistamine properties toward hay fever.

Genistein and other isoflavones from soy products are being investigated for their anticancer effects. Soy products have long been associated with the Japanese diet which has been recognized as a particularly healthy one overall.

Carotenoids

These were probably the first phytochemicals to be recognized, with beta carotene, the orange pigment that gives color to carrots, most well known. Like beta carotene, many carotenoids are also potent antioxidants. Lycopene, found in tomatoes, grapefruits, and watermelons, is a red pigment that appears to be more active in foods that have been processed and cooked. It may prevent many cancers including cervical, prostate, as well as lowering LDL cholesterol levels in the blood.

A reasonable intake has been linked with a 50 per cent reduction in the incidence of heart attacks.

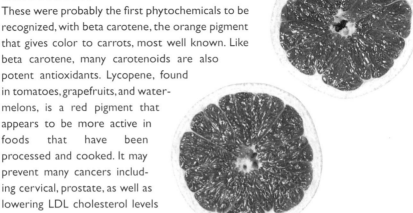

Grapefruit contains lots of lycopene— a carotenoid.

Lutein and zeaxanthin are carotenoids present in healthy retinas. Retinas are the membranes in the eye that have light and color receptors that enable us to see. Spinach and kale have high levels of lutein and it is abundant in many other fruits and vegetables, but the highest levels are found in egg yolks and maize. The combination of lutein and other essential vitamins is beneficial to those at risk from macular degeneration, particularly the elderly.

Glucosinolates

These compounds act as natural pesticides and were thought to be toxic to humans. They are found mainly in green vegetables, particularly cruciforms such as cabbage, Brussels sprouts, cauliflower, and kale.

Cauliflowers are a good source of glucosinolates which are thought to have an anticancer effect.

Broccoli and cauliflower are rich sources of glucosinolates that break down to sulphoraphane, a substance that has a strong anticancer effect by stimulating the body's own natural defenses. Singrin, present in Brussels sprouts, has been found to suppress the growth of pre-cancerous cells, while isothio-cyanate found in watercress, can render one of the main cancer-causing agents in tobacco smoke harmless.

Indoles, found in sprouts and broccoli, have been found to be helpful in fighting hormone related cancers.

Organosulfides

Members of the allium family, that is onions, garlic, leeks, and chives, are the main sources of these sulfides, which are known to stimulate the immune system. They are also antioxidants and have a role in fighting cancers, ulcers, and heart disease. In particular, garlic is a rich source of allicin, a well-known antibiotic and antiviral. It also contains diallyl sulfide, which appears to shrink cancerous tumors, while the other phy-tochemicals help to prevent pre-cancerous cells developing, as well has having roles in reducing LDL cholesterol and preventing blood clots.

Garlic is well known for its ability to protect against minor infections and colds, but also for its odor. Alliin is an odorless compound found in intact garlic cloves. When a clove is crushed, alliin reacts with the enzyme alliinase to form allicin, which acts as a natural insecticide to the plant. This is an unstable compound that quickly converts to other chemicals. There are a variety of products on the market that provide the wonders of garlic in capsule form, and many now proclaim they are odor free.

Phytoestrogens

As their name implies, these substance have chemical formulas similar to estrogen, the female hormone known to protect against heart disease and osteoporosis. Phytoestrogens appear to be linked with reduction in the risk of hormone dependent cancers. There are two main types: isoflavones and lignans.

Garlic is a wonderful all-round health-giving plant. It contains sulfides which may prevent cancers and act as an antioxidant to lower blood cholesterol.

Isoflavones can be acquired from pulses, in particular soya beans. Research has shown that a high intake of soya correlates to a low incidence of breast cancer development with the compound equol having the best effect. Soya is often advocated for use by women going through the menopause and it is the isoflavones that are thought to reduce hot flushes and night sweats.

Lignans can be found in flax seeds, whole grains, and berries. Enterolactone is a potent lignan that would appear to be beneficial in preventing breast cancer.

Other important phytochemicals are:

• **Bromelian** (found in pineapples) aids digestion and has a blood thinning property.

• **Papain** (found in papaya) also aids digestion and acts as a pain reliever.

• **Capsaicin** (found in chilies) has anti-inflammatory properties, is an antioxidant and pain reliever, and can reduce LDL blood cholesterol.

• **Resveratrol** are present in red grape juice and red wine, and protects against coronary heart disease.

• **Coumarins** (found in fruit, vegetables, and licorice) help to thin the blood and may play a role in preventing stroke and coronary heart disease. In medicine it is better known as warfarin and is the most commonly used oral anticoagulant medication.

• **Saponin** is an effective anticancer, antimicrobial, and cholesterol-lowering phytochemical. Digitalis is an example used as heart medications.

Bromelian found in pineapples is said to have many properties; it may relieve the symptoms of angina, reduce joint inflammation of arthritis, and aid tissue repair.

Red wine has resveratrol which protects against heart disease.

SUMMARY OF FOOD SOURCES AND PHYTOCHEMICALS

Plant source	Phytochemicals
Artichoke	Silymarin, cynarin
Beans, grains, and seeds including soybeans, oats, barley, brown rice, whole wheat	Flavonoids/isoflavones (coumesterol found in soy products), saponins, protease inhibitors
Broccoli, cauliflower, cabbage, Brussels sprouts, kale, turnips, bok choy, kohlrabi	Indoles/glucosinolates (potent anticancer properties), sulfaforaphane, isothiocyanates/thiocyanates, thiols
Carrots, celery, cilantro, parsley, parsnips	Carotenoids, phthalides (butyl phthalide is found in celery), polyacetylenes
Garlic, onions, chives, leeks	Allyl sulfides (allicin, ajoene in garlic)
Grapes, berries, cherries, apples, pears, cantaloupe, watermelon, pomegranate	Ellagic acid (natural pesticide), phenols, flavonoids (quercetin)

Plant source	Phytochemicals
Herbs and spices i.e. ginger, mint, rosemary, thyme, oregano, sage, basil, tumeric, caraway, fennel	Gingerols, flavonoids, monoterpenes (limonene)
Licorice root, green tea, red wine	Glycyrrhizin, catechins (catechin hydrate found in tea), polyphenols
Oranges, lemons, lime, grapefruit	Carotenoids, glucarates monoterpenes (limonene)
Tomatoes, bell peppers, egg plants, potatoes	Lycopene (protects against heart disease and other disorders)

Globe artichokes contain a compound cynarin, which is thought to boost liver function and regulate blood cholesterol. It may also help irritable bowel syndrome.

A lot of plants contain useful amounts of beta carotene and fennel is no exception.

SUPPLEMENTS

If you live in an urban environment, smoke, have high exposure to x-rays or sunlight, are stressed, or have started to notice wrinkles on your skin, you should seriously consider your antioxidant intake. This book advocates that the best way to get a boost from antioxidants and phytochemicals is to acquire them through food. You should be very wary when using single supplements as some of the doses recommended can have adverse effects. Plant flavonoids actually have the capacity to become carcinogenic at higher levels. The levels available in some supplements are much higher than you could acquire through eating: the volume of food you would have to eat to get the equivalent amount would be enormous! However the jury is still out on which people would fully benefit from taking supplements. Some researchers have claimed that the elderly (especially those with a reduced food intake), frequent aspirin takers, heavy drinkers, smokers, and people with impaired immune systems may benefit from taking daily antioxidant supplements. With regard to heart disease and stroke, it is possible that higher levels of antioxidants slow or prevent the development of arterial blockages by having an effect on the oxidation of cholesterol and they may deter the collection of plaque on arterial walls.

A general antioxidant supplement may be a good protective measure. Lifestyles today mean that eating the recommended number of portions of fruit and vegetables is not always possible, but it cannot be stated enough that a supplement can never compensate for a poor diet.

As long as you take the supplements as directed, antioxidants are generally safe. Many multivitamins are marketed as having antioxidant factors. The following quantities are guidelines for a typical formulation: 10–15mg beta carotene, 150mg or more of vitamin C, 100IU of vitamin E, 50–200µg selenium. In addition 5–15mg of zinc with other nutrients involved in the antioxidant defense system—copper, manganese, and 1-cysteine (an amino acid)—are sometimes added.

Other useful supplements

Some herbal substances are also known to have antioxidant functions, for instance ginkgo bilboa. They may be included in a supplement, but they are probably better taken in separate herbal formulations in order to be properly effective. The leaves of the ginkgo bilboa tree are not something we'd normally munch on, but supplements are made of ground-up dried leaves or extracts of the active ingredients from the leaves; the nuts are also available at

Gingko bilboa's main active ingredient is flavone glycoisides which is extracted from the leaves, but small amounts may be present in the nuts.

specialist outlets. Traditionally ginkgo nuts are distributed at Japanese weddings. The active ingredients are said to have an effect on brain-power, particularly memory and concentration and increases the blood supply to the fingers and toes.

Another antioxidant preparation you might see is the enzyme superoxide dismutase. This works in conjunction with the enzyme catalase and is known to disarm and destroy free radicals, par-ticularly superoxide. Although there have been claims that taking supplements is beneficial to forestall or reduce the effects of aging these have not been proven yet. It is likely to be destroyed in the diges-tive system if taken orally. The functioning of cytosolic superoxide dismutase requires copper and zinc.

Co-enzyme Q10

Co-enzyme Q10, although an antioxidant, has other important func-tions. Discovered in 1857, it is also known as ubiquinone (from the latin meaning everywhere) or CoQ10 and is found in every cell in the body.

As we age our production of this substance drops off, although it is found in foods, but processing can destroy it. Especially good food sources are meat (including poultry), fish including macker-el and sardines, whole grains, nuts, spinach, broccoli, and vegetable oils. CoQ10 takes part in the metabolic pathway that creates adenosine triphosphate (ATP) in the cells. This is the basic unit of power in cells and provides the energy which drives all the functions performed by the cells. CoQ10 levels are highest in the organs that have the biggest energy requirements, such as the heart. It also plays a part in out immune system, stimulating white cell production to fight off attacking germs, and consequently we have a higher requirement for it during and after an infection.

Supplements of CoQ10 are better taken separately and are said to help the body convert food into energy, act as an antioxidant, and reduce hot flushes, but many nutritionists feel the case for supplements is unproven. It would appear to be safe in doses up to 150mg without toxic effects, but care should be taken if you are also taking blood-thinning drugs. Angina and heart patients apparently benefit from supplements, which improve cardiac function. Research in US and Japan has also shown that there is a positive benefit to those who suffer from hypertension.

WHAT EFFECT CAN ANTIOXIDANTS HAVE ON YOUR LIFE?

Reduce the risk of heart disease

Research has shown that higher consumption of vitamin E, and to a less extent beta carotene, can be associated with a reduction in the rate of coronary arterial disease. Studies from Cambridge University show that cardiac patients given a vitamin E supplement daily had their risk of non-fatal heart attacks reduced by 75 percent. Co-enzyme Q10 and flavonoids such as quercetin, rutin, and catechin have also been shown to be protective against coronary disease.

Nuts are excellent sources of antioxidant phytochemicals.

153

The glycosides in asparagus may have anti-inflammatory properties
that are useful for the treatment of arthritis.

Perk up fertility

Vitamin C has been shown to reduce the number of genetic abnormal-
ities in the sperm of heavy smokers when taken daily. Daily vitamin E
improves the ability of sperm to attach to the egg.

Low levels of selenium are associated with the increased
risk of miscarriage.

Protect the skin

Results show that carotenoids increase sun protection: antioxidants
and PABA applied in sunscreen may slow wrinkle formation.

Healthy pregnancy

Studies have shown a link between poor antioxidant status and a high
risk of pre-eclampsia.

Reduce cancer risk

Antioxidants play a major role in reducing cancers of all organs.
University of California studies report that high intakes of antioxidants
can reduce the chance of getting cancer by half. Arizona Cancer Center
found patients with skin cancer who were placed on daily supplements
of selenium had a 50 percent reduced risk of dying from cancer.
However, it would appear that antioxidants work together mopping up
carcinogenic free radicals to produce the most beneficial effects. Beta
carotene and vitamins C and E are indicated.

Boost immunity

Beta carotene and vitamin C increase the efficiency of the immune system. Low selenium levels in HIV patients increase risk of developing
AIDS. Vitamin E offsets many age-related declines in immunity.

Preventing eye disease

UVB light has been shown to play a role in cataract formation and antioxidants have a protective effect. Carotenoids can thicken the macular pigment of the retina; lutein and zeaxanthin are highly protective against macular degeneration. Harvard University reports vitamin C supplements reduce the risk of cataracts by 83 percent over 10 years.

Improving respiratory function

Lungs heavily exposed to the oxidative effect of smog and smoke can lead to diseases such as asthma, emphysema, and acute respiratory distress syndrome. Antioxidant therapy is suggested for relief. St Thomas' Hospital, London, reported that high pollution compromises the antioxidant status of epithelial lining fluid in the lungs and that vitamins E and C benefit asthmatics exposed to pollution.

Protect from exercise damage

With regular exercise you will breathe deeper taking in more oxygen and so producing oxidants which can cause muscle damage. A diet high in antioxidants will help counter the effects.

Counteracting a high fat diet

After a high fat meal the level of blood fats in blood vessel walls increases. It does not increase after either a low fat meal or a high fat meal with added antioxidants.

Most exercise is good for us, but if you exercise outdoors, think about your antioxidant needs and other nutritional requirements that can help keep you in top form.

4. PROTEIN AND AMINO ACIDS

You may have heard it said that proteins and amino acids are the building blocks of life and it really is true. Nothing exists in nature without amino acids and they are the constituents of proteins as well as, more importantly, the life molecule DNA.

PROTEINS

Proteins are complex organic compounds found in all living cells, and so they are the most abundant class of all biological molecules. The constituent elements of most proteins are carbon, hydrogen, oxygen, and in most cases, sulfur. Some also incorporate copper, iron, phosphorous, and zinc. Proteins are made up of different amounts of the same 22 amino acids, which are united through chemical links called peptide bonds. Linked together the amino acids form polypeptide chains. The order in which the amino acids are arranged gives rise to specific proteins. The physiological activity of most proteins is also closely linked to their three-dimensional structure.

Proteins are needed in the diet mostly for their component amino acids, which the body uses to build new proteins. Proteins can be found everywhere and are easy to get in your diet. They are essential for growth and development in children, cell maintenance and repair, and regulation of many body functions.

Left: When protein comes packaged like this who can resist?

Proteins are divided into two major classes based upon chemical structure: simple proteins, which are composed of only amino acids, and conjugated proteins, which have amino acids and additional chemical groups. Conjugated proteins include glycoproteins, which contain carbohydrates (sugars); lipoproteins, which contain lipids (fats); and nucleoproteins, which contain nucleic acids i.e. DNA (full name deoxyribose nucleic acid).

All meats are packed with protein, but watch out for saturated fats in products like this.

Many proteins have important biological functions and can be classified into the following groups:

• enzymes, which are responsible for catalyzing the chemical reactions in living cells;

• structural proteins such as keratin, elastin, and collagen. Keratin is a constituent protein of hair, skin (particularly in the palms and soles of the feet), and fingernails. Elastin and collagen are major component of bone, muscle, and connective tissue;

• gas transport proteins i.e. hemoglobin;

• nutrient molecules i.e. casein and ovalbumin (found in eggs);

• antibodies, which are important molecules of the immune system;

• protein hormones, which regulate metabolism;

• proteins that perform "mechanical" work, such as actin and myosin, muscle proteins.

ENZYMES

We must say a short word about enzymes here, especially as you have probably heard something about them. They are absolutely vital to the proper functioning of cell metabolism. Enzymes are globular (conjugated) proteins.

Animals are fueled by the intake of organic food, which is degraded by the digestion process to turn it into useful molecular materials which can be used to provide energy and nutrients to the body. There are two main metabolic processes at the cellular level

Eggs are a useful addition to any diet, packed with protein and minerals.

happening during the digestive process: the first extracts energy from food stuffs and channels the resultant energy into useful functions, and the second is the chemical alteration and rearrangement of nutrient molecules to form other biologically useful molecules. The production of amino acids from protein sources is an example of the first process. The creation of new protein molecules from amino acids is an example of the second process.

At all stages of the metabolic digestion process catalysts are required. The catalysts of the biological world are enzymes. They frequently require the presence of certain inorganic minerals (which act as cofactors), such as magnesium, sodium, potassium, chlorine, or calcium, to help regulate the enzyme function.

Enzymes work only for specific reactions, and with particular substrates. That is, in order to digest our various foods, we require specific enzymes to help break the complex food into its chemical components. Enzymes reduce the energy required to digest food, by increasing the rate at which various chemical reactions take place to split the food into its component molecules. Different enzymes work in different sections of the digestive tract; some require particular conditions in which to work efficiently. For instance, in the body one enzyme which dismantles protein to amino acids is called pepsin. Secreted in the stomach it requires the presence of hydrochloric acid (which ensures the pH is kept low at a value of about two) to work effectively. In later stages along the gut other enzymes also work on the polypeptide chains of proteins: trypsin secreted from the pancreas goes to work on food in the duodenum; peptidases secreted from the gut lining act in the small intestine.

Your body does not have a finite supply of enzymes: they are manufactured as needed from the amino acids in the diet. Enzyme supplement tablets and other preparations will probably not aid the digestive process in any way as they will undoubtedly be broken down

*The main sugar in milk is lactose, which a few
percentage of people cannot tolerate.*

into their constituent amino acids in the stomach and gut. They may contribute to your overall amino acid intake, but only minutely. If you are eating a balanced and nutritious diet there should be no insufficiency of enzymes in your body to deal with the complex molecules of your food.

There is one enzyme however that some adults cannot manufacture in adequate quantities. Lactose is the main carbohydrate in milk, and people with insufficient amounts of the enzyme lactase are unable to digest it; they will experience diarrhea, bloating, and cramps after consuming foods and beverages containing lactose. There are products on the market which contain the enzyme lactase which can be used to aid in dairy product digestion. There are exceptions to the "supplementary enzymes will be digested" rule.

Lactase insufficiency is quite a well-known disorder, but there are some other diseases, for example, cystic fibrosis, where the body is unable to produce enough digestive enzymes in the pancreas. Some of the most important enzymes are produced here; insulin is secreted to the blood while pancreatic juices contain lipases to digest fats, proteases to digest proteins, and amylases to digest starches. In such cases where their manufacture is inadequate enzyme replacement therapy is indicated, but a doctor will diagnose the disorder, and prescribe appropriate medication. Prescription enzymes tablets are specially coated to withstand the high acidity of the stomach and to dissolve once in the small intestine, where they set to work.

AMINO ACIDS

As noted above, proteins and enzymes are composed of a series of linked amino acids. Amino acids are classified as essential and non-essential. Of the 22 amino acids which are all crucial to life, eight are essential (highlighted in bold in the list). Essential amino acids cannot be manufactured within the body and must be obtained from food. Non-essential amino acids can be synthesized from an excess of the others. Histidine is considered essential only for infants and children.

Alanine
Arginine
Asparagine
Aspartic acid
Cysteine
Cystine
Glutamic acid
Glutamine
Glycine
Histidine
Isoleucine
Leucine
Lysine
Methione
Ornithine
Phenylalanine
Proline
Serine
Threonine
Tryptophan
Tyrosine
Valine

So that the body can successfully produce any necessary proteins and enzymes, all the essential amino acids must be present in the right quantities. The absence of just one amino acid can adversely affect protein synthesis. If an essential amino acid is low or missing it impacts the effectiveness of the others. The amino acids are used in different combinations to make different proteins, for instance muscle.

PROTEINS AND NUTRITION

Proteins—a collective term for a lot of compounds. Nutritionally, proteins are grouped into two main types: first class or complete, and second class or incomplete. First class or complete protein provides the full range of essential amino acids and can be obtained from meat, poultry, seafood, eggs, milk, and cheese. Second class or incomplete proteins don't contain the full range of amino acids, and are best eaten with other foods, particularly animal sourced protein. This second type of protein is found in nuts, seeds, grains, and beans. A mix of both types of protein is best for an adequate uptake of essential amino acids.

When we exercise, our bodies make new muscle fibers and we need amino acids to do this.

You may be surprised to learn that proteins provide just as many calories as carbohydrate. Gram for gram the calorie count is the same:

1g protein	= 4 calories
1g carbohydrate	= 4 calories
1g fat	= 9 calories

So how much protein should we be getting in our diets? WHO figures estimate that we should get 10–15 percent of our daily calories from protein, and most people in developed countries can manage up 13–20 percent easily. There are apparent health disadvantages to consuming a very high protein diet. It is not recommended for diabetics as it may exacerbate kidney problems and there is evidence that it is dangerous to kidney function in the long-term. Excess protein in the blood is filtered out by the kidneys and if not used to build and repair muscle tissue, is converted to energy or stored as fat. High protein intake has also been linked with bone demineralization—it causes calcium to be excreted in urine—so it may be important for women, and those at risk from osteoporosis, to include less, or no more than 15 percent protein in a daily diet. A small number of studies are building up a body of evidence that show high protein intake may be linked to high blood pressure too.

Enthusiasts of a higher protein diet believe that it is a more natural way for us to eat, and better for our metabolism. This is how our ancestors in millions of year ago ate, and interestingly it is probably how most

A source of first class protein, and tasty too.

The protein requirements of young children are not surprising,
considering how active and curious they can be!

indigenous peoples ate until the 19th century too. However, there is insufficient evidence that we should greatly increase our protein intake from the recommended levels at present.

How much protein should we eat?

As a general rule, you should aim to include 0.015oz per pound (0.75g per kg) of body weight. It should be noted, however, that the older we get, the less we need. A toddler's daily protein requirement is about two-and-a-half times greater than an adult's because of their rapid pace of growth and development. Any protein that is surplus to the requirements of the body's processes can be converted to glucose and used for energy.

Good sources of proteins

As we've already mentioned, we get a full complement of essential amino acids from the proteins from animal sources, that is meat, poultry, seafood, eggs, milk, and cheese. Soybeans, quinoa (a grain), and spinach are also considered to provide an adequate supply of essential amino acids. Second class proteins found in nuts, seeds, grains, and beans need to be eaten in addition to foods whose proteins supply the missing amino acids. Protein sources of non-animal origin usually have all of the essential amino acids, but the amounts of one or two of these amino acids may be low. For example, grains are low in lysine and legumes (that is beans and peas) are low in methionine—both essential amino acids—when compared to foods of high quality protein.

For many people meat is still their main source of protein.

Tofu and other soy products are essential protein sources for vegetarian diets.

Overall we would all benefit from eating more plant-based protein, as this has the added benefit of adding phyto-chemicals, fiber, and complex carbohydrate to our diet too. It is important to remember to choose less saturated fat in the diet: fish is an excellent low fat source of animal protein, while meat such as beef and lamb have higher levels of saturated fat.

VEGETARIANS AND VEGANS

A good vegetarian diet is generally very healthy, as the intake of foods bursting with phytochemicals, antioxidants, fiber, vitamin C etc. is higher than a meat eater's diet. It's probably also higher in unsaturated fats and essential fatty acids. It should be noted that the positive benefits of this diet can be achieved by non-vegetarians too, if they eat a higher proportion of fruit and vegetables, and reduce the amount of dairy produce consumed. Vegans, who eat no dairy produce at all and nothing from an animal source, have a diet that is consequently highly restricted. However, research shows that their protein intake is 75 percent of the average. Since vegans eat a variety of plant protein sources, their RDA for protein should be between 0.015oz and 0.019oz per pound (0.75g and 1.0g per kilo) of body weight.

Legumes are one way to add variety to a diet. They also contain quercertin, a flavonoid that plays a role in preventing coronary heart disease.

For a while it has been thought that most plant proteins were "incomplete"—with the exception of soy products. How do vegetarians and vegans get their full complement of amino acids? Well, the best way is by having a varied diet, one that includes grains, pulses, tofu, nuts, and seeds as well as leafy vegetables. Vegetarians who eat dairy produce such as cheese and eggs probably won't need to take any supplements. A better way is to eat different protein sources to obtain the essentials; by eating a variety of unrefined grains, legumes, seeds, nuts, and vegetables throughout the day, if one food is low in a particular essential amino acid, another food will make up the shortfall.

PROTEIN SUPPLEMENTS

I'm sure we've all heard of protein supplements, especially in connection with invalids or those convalescing from illness who need "building up" and in relation to athletic activities. For people unable to gain their full complement of protein from whole foods, protein supplements may be beneficial. The better formulas are derived from soybeans and are available as a liquid or powder, without added carbohydrates and fats.

The supplements can be added to drinks or food. Protein supplements are seen by some nutritionists as expensive, unnecessary, and even harmful for some people, therefore we would recommend that you always consult your health practitioner for advice before adding them to your diet.

Most of us could do with getting more plant based protein, and benefit from the micronutrients present in a range of vegetables.

AMINO ACID SUPPLEMENTS

Amino acid supplements are not recommended for pregnant women, children, diabetics, and those with high blood pressure. Many individual amino acid supplements are available but the scientific evidence to support their effectiveness is not vast. Some practitioners believe that they can do many things from boosting the immune system to reducing the dependency on drugs. As stated above, all proteins break down to form amino acids, so to get the full complement naturally eat protein-rich foods. Always consult your health practitioner before taking any supplements.

If you take an amino acid supplement, make sure it contains the eight essential amino acids or it is a waste of money. Amino acids in crystalline form will be absorbed directly into the blood stream.

The RDA of essential amino acids for adults, per kilogram of body weight per day: isoleucine 10mg; leucine 14mg; lysine 12mg; methionine 13mg; phenylalanine 14mg; threonine 7mg; tryptophan 3.5mg; valine 10mg. Infants also need histidine 28mg.

The following is a summary of information for a few of the more commonly found amino acid supplements.

ARGININE is an amino acid is necessary for normal function of the pituitary gland in the brain and required for synthesis of human growth hormone. It is a constituent of seminal fluid, and is needed for male fertility.

Good for: sperm count, aids immune response and healing, metabolism of stored fat.

Best natural source: brown rice, carob, chocolate, gelatin, nuts, oatmeal, popcorn, raisins, sunflower seeds, sesame seeds, whole wheat bread.

ASPARTIC ACID aids with the disposal of the chemical ammonia. This is a toxic waste product that is converted to urea before excretion in urine. Research indicates that this amino acid may be important in giving increased resistance against fatigue; indeed one study showed that when athletes were given salts of aspartic acid, it much improved their levels of stamina and endurance.

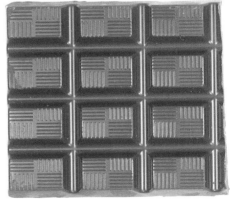

Many chocoholics will be pleased to note the beneficial effects of its arginine content but most chocolate is a good source of calcium too.

CYSTEINE and CYSTINE are two amino acids that are readily converted from one into the other as the body requires; cystine is the more stable form. Together they are valuable in protecting the body from free radicals, particularly those associated with smoking and drinking. Along with **methionine** they are believed to offer protection against excess copper. Some research has shown that therapeutic supplements of cysteine can offer some protection against x-ray and nuclear radiation.

GLUTAMINE and GLUTAMIC ACID are used as a source of energy in the brain. It mops up excess ammonia (a toxic waste product of cell metabolism) in the blood converting it to glutamine. Glutamine has been indicated in helping control alcoholism, alleviating fatigue, depression, and impotence. Interestingly, it also has a role in intelligence, and has been used effectively in the treatment of senility and schizophrenia.

GLYCINE is a favorite of nutrition doctors for use in the treatment of hypoglycemia (low blood sugar). It apparently stimulates the release of glucagon to mobilize glucogen which is converted to glucose. Also seen to be useful in the treatment of low pituitary function and by supplying additional creatine which is essential for muscle formation. It is also been used successfully to treat academia (low pH of the blood), in particular a type caused by a leucine imbalance which results in very unpleasant body odor.

LYSINE is an essential amino acid needed for growth and repair of tissues. Intimately involved in the production of hormones, enzymes, and antibodies. Older people, particularly men, require more lysine than younger ones.

Good for: promotes better concentration, alleviates some fertility problems.

Best natural sources: cheese, eggs, fish, lima beans, meat, milk, soy products, and yeast.

METHIONE

Apparently has a role in lowering the amount of histamine in the blood. In conjunction with choline and folic acid it appears to offer protection against some tumors.

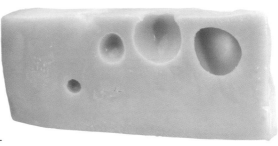

Cheese is not only a good source of lysine, but full of useful vitamins and minerals too.

ORNITHINE Together with **arginine**, ornithine is involved with the release of human growth hormone. Ornithine stimulates the secretion of insulin and research has indicated it has a role in increasing the amount of arginine in the body. Some people believe that because growth hormone (which is secreted when you sleep) acts as a mobilizer of fat that ornithine and arginine can help you "diet in your sleep," and as a result they are popular supplements.

PHENYLALANINE is an essential amino acid. Phenylalanine acts as a neurotransmitter and is a precursor to noradrenaline and dopamine.

Good for: Reduces hunger, increases sexual interest, improves memory and mental alertness, alleviates depression.

Best natural source: Almonds, cottage cheese, dry skimmed milk, lima beans, peanuts, pumpkin and sesame seeds, protein rich foods, and soy products.

Phenylalanine is converted into tyrosine, except in some people with the inherited disorder phenylketonuria (PKU). The intake of phenylalanine should be restricted in these cases, and generally a low protein diet is followed.

DL-PHENYLALANINE

(DLPA) is a mixture of the natural (L) and synthetic (D) forms of phenylalanine. It is believed to be a natural pain killer that is particularly active for conditions such as whiplash, osteo- and rheumatoid arthritis, lower back pain, migraines, muscle cramps, post-operative pain, and neuralgia. Check with a doctor before taking it.

All nuts have a high protein content.

TRYPTOPHAN is an essential amino acid. Along with B6, niacin, and magnesium, it is used to create serotonin, a neurotransmitter. Serotonin takes part in a wide range of body functions including blood clotting, blood pressure, and it has a role in natural body rhythms, associated with the day-night cycle (circadian rhythms).

Good for: Induces natural sleep, reducing pain sensitivity, natural antidepressant, reducing anxiety and tension.

Best natural source: Bananas, cottage cheese, dried dates, fish, milk, meat, peanuts, turkey, lettuce, and protein-rich foods.

TYROSINE is an important neurotransmitter with a role in stimulating and modifying brain activity.

Remember the tale of Peter Rabbit who fell asleep after eating too many lettuces? It was the tryptophan!

5. FAT AND FAT MANIPULATORS

Fat is one of the essential macronutrients needed in all diets. Although we tend to associate "fat" with "bad" when it comes to food, it is really an essential component. While it's true that not all fat is bad, some types are definitely better than others. A more technical term used by many scientists and nutritionists is the word lipids. You may also have heard of fatty acids, polyunsaturated fat, monounsaturated fat, lipotropics…we'll get to them all shortly.

WHAT IS FAT?

Fat is a generic term for a group of chemicals used by plants and animals as a source of energy. In animals, fat is found as adipose (fatty) tissue around various organs and joints and under the skin. Fat is used as a reserve fuel, as a shock absorber and insulator. Its distribution in men and women is related to function: in men, fat is stored on the abdomen and is quickly accessed and easily utilized energy; in women, fat tends to be stored around the hips and thighs and is better for releasing energy stores steadily during pregnancy and when breast feeding. In plants, fat is found in the stems, seeds, and fruits in the form of oil. (Oil and fat are terms that we use to describe the state of the lipid: oil is liquid at room temperature; fat is solid.)

Of the components of a healthy diet most nutritionists suggest that we should get no more that 35 percent of our daily energy

Left: Butter is what we all think fat looks like but there are other sources.

Fats that are liquid at room temperature are oils,
and some are better for you than others.

from fat, yet in the Western world we regularly manage to exceed this. Fat provides twice as many calories per gram than either protein or carbohydrate, and if it is not used it is stored as adipose tissue. This can be accessed easily later on when needed.

Fat is needed in the diet to help us absorb fat-soluble vitamins (A, D, E) and we require a supply of fatty acids, the breakdown product of fat. Fatty acids are used in the production of chemicals such as prostaglandins that are involved in blood clotting and hormonal responses. However, high fat diets have been liked with heart disease, some forms of cancer, obesity, and ill health. The proportion of obese people is on the rise in western countries, and as a consequence the number of people making demands on medical services in relation to diet related health problems. If we learn to sort out the good fats from the bad fats, as well as reducing our overall intake, we could reap many positive benefits.

THE SCIENCE BIT

Fat is composed of units of glycerol and fatty acids. Fats are emulsified by the action of bile and pancreatic juice in the intestine. The components (glycerol and fatty acids) are absorbed by the lymphatic system before entering the blood stream. When fat stores are broken down, they yield fatty acids. Fat stores are in a constant state of flux; fat is being laid down and utilized so there is a continual supply of fatty acid available for use. The regulation of lipids in the body is directed by the liver; fat is either utilized for energy or sent to the adipose (fat) stores.

The type of fat consumed can have a major impact on our lives. Fatty acids can be divided into three groups: saturated fatty acids (SFA), polyunsaturated fatty acids (PUFA), and monounsaturated fatty acids

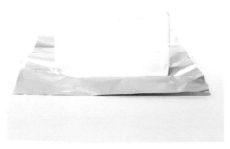

Although there is some monounsaturated fat, butter is mostly saturated fat.

(MUFA). All food contains the three types, but in differing proportions. We may all think butter is saturated fat, but about 25 percent is MUFA. In general, butter, milk, and other animal products have higher proportions of saturated fatty acids. We know that SFA can raise the level of cholesterol in the blood, which could lead to arteriosclerosis, hence they are the seen as the "bad" fats. Unsaturated fats (PUFA and MUFA) found in vegetable oils can reduce high levels of blood cholesterol, and are seen as being better.

SATURATED FAT

Saturated fats are usually solid at room temperature and are found primarily in animal sources. Sources of saturated fat include, visible fat on meat, cheese, cream, milk, eggs, butter, lard, tropical oils such as palm and coconut oils, and in a variety of manufactured pies, cakes, and cookies. The amount of fat in meat can be significantly less if the animal is pasture fed, and levels are then nearer to those found in poultry and game: grain fed animals produce "marbled" meat which may taste good, but the marbling is saturated fat. Interestingly, when people stop eating meat and eat a vegetarian diet, they

The marbling of meat may add to the flavor, but it is all saturated fat.

Coconut fat is not like animal saturated fat and so isn't a risk for heart disease.

often replace meat with a lot of dairy produce and so still eat just as much saturated fat as meat eaters do.

A diet with a large amount of saturated fat can raise the levels of LDL cholesterol in the blood (see notes on cholesterol further on). This is linked with an increase in heart disease, and other problems including obesity and cancer. It is also thought that saturate fats compete with the essential fats and may prevent them from being effective within the body. It is recommended that only 10 percent of our total fat intake should be saturated fat.

POLYUNSATURATED FAT

Most types of polyunsaturated fat are liquid at room temperature. Many, but not all, vegetable oils are polyunsaturated: corn, safflower,

Sunflower seeds are a great source of polyunsaturated fat.

sunflower oil, walnut oil, and many nuts are particularly good as they are high in essential fatty acids. We need about 18 percent of our daily fat intake to be polyunsaturated. They have a lowering effect on LDL cholesterol levels but are also known to be easily oxidized in the body forming free radicals—substances that have been implicated in the formation of cancers and other diseases. A diet high in antioxidants will counter this. PUFAs are also a rich source of vitamin E.

ESSENTIAL FATTY ACIDS

Essential fatty acids are fats that we can't synthesize. While we can synthesize most fatty acids needed by our bodies from the products of protein and carbohydrate metabolism, there are certain essential unsaturated fatty acids—for example linoleic and linolenic acids—that we must get from our diet. Only small amounts are required and the best sources are vegetable and seed oils. If we get enough linoleic acid we can synthesize the other essential fatty acids. While the in-depth functions of fatty acids are not completely understood, shortage can result in retarded growth, reproductive deficiency, and kidney failure.

Vitamin F is a collective term for the unsaturated linoleic, linolenic, and arachidonic fatty acids. Unsaturated fats aid the metabolism of saturated fat, and it's a good idea to include them if you have a heavy carbohydrate intake.

Just to make things slightly more confusing, the essential fatty acids have alternative names. Linoleic acid is one of the n-6 group of PUFAs and is often called omega-6; alpha linolenic acid is one of the n-3 group of PUFAs and is known as omega-3. The best sources of omega-6 and omega-3 are vegetables, oils, almonds, avocados, linseeds, peanuts, pecans, rapeseeds, and sunflower seeds. Research has shown that a diet

*Salmon is one of several oily fish, including herring and mackerel,
that are appetizing sources of essential fatty acids.*

which includes sufficient essential fatty acids may help and control a variety of ills: arthritis, cancer, heart disease, many immune system conditions, and skin complaints.

One of the omega-6 oils that have been researched is gamma-linolenic acid (GLA). This can be produced in the body from linolenic acid, but one of the best-known sources is evening primrose oil (EPO). It is needed for the production of prostaglandins. EPO supplements are often used by women to alleviate premenstrual syndrome and menopausal symptoms, but EPO is also useful in the treatment of the skin condition eczema.

There are two omega-3 oils that are of importance. Eicosapentanoic acid (EPA) and docosahexanoic acid (DHA). These are found in oily fish and fish oils, such as mackerel, sardines, herring, salmon, fresh tuna, and trout. Studies have shown that they reduce the stickiness of blood, reducing its tendency to clot: this is important in preventing coronary heart disease and stroke. In addition they may also help beat depression and improve brainpower. DHA is a vital component of brain tissue, and accumulates in fetal brains during the last three months of pregnancy. Lack of DHA at this time can impair the child's learning ability.

TRANS FAT

Trans fats are fats that have been altered. Most trans fat in our diet are saturated fats that have hydrogenated, or altered, while being processed and become hard at room temperature—margarine is one example. The hydrogenated fats behave like saturated fats in the body, but

Look on the side of any pack of margarine to see the list of hydrogenated fats that are its main constituents.

187

there is evidence that they are a bit worse. In addition to raising LDL cholesterol levels they also lower HDL levels—a bit of a double whammy. We should limit our intake to about six percent of our total fat intake. Trans fats can be found in hard cooking fats, but also in commercially produced puddings, cakes, cookies, and in some takeout meals.

MONOUNSATURATED FAT

Monounsaturated fats are usually liquid at room temperature, although they may become solid if chilled—like putting olive oil in the fridge, for instance. They are found in many nuts, avocados, rapeseed oil, olive oil, and olives. Initially they were thought not to have an effect on cholesterol blood levels but they are now known to be much better than PUFAs. Not only do MUFAs lower LDL levels but they also help to maintain the levels of HDL. A Mediterranean diet is the example often quoted as being high in MUFA. It is linked with lower levels of heart disease and longevity. Oils that are high in MUFA also tend to have high levels of vitamin E too.

Monounsaturated fats should make up the greater percentage of our fat intake: about 36 percent overall, but it could be more than this if you eliminate the saturated and trans fats. This could be achieved by altering your diet to include more plant-based foods, and fewer animals-based products and processed foods.

CHOLESTEROL

Cholesterol is found in many foods of animal origin and rarely in plants. A smooth waxy substance it is an important component of cell membranes, and is stored in the adrenals, ovaries, and testes where it is converted to steroid hormones. These hormones include sex hormones (androgens and estrogens), as well as the adrenal corticoids,

Hazelnuts and macadamia nuts are high in MUFAs.

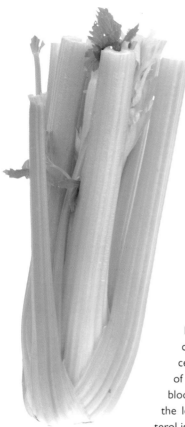

cortisol, corticosterone, and aldosterones. Cholesterol is the precursor of several bile acids produced in the liver but any excess is usually excreted in bile although it can precipitate to form gallstones. If is there is surplus cholesterol in the blood, it may be deposited in the arteries as plaque. This eventually obstructs the smooth flow of blood and may form a clot which may lead to a heart attack or stroke.

In the blood, fats are known as lipoproteins. There are four groups: chylomicrons, very low density lipoproteins (VLDL), high density lipoproteins (HDL), and low density lipoproteins (LDL). LDLs and VLDLs contain large amounts of cholesterol which they carry through the blood and deposit in cells. HDLs pick up the cholesterol and carry it to the liver for processing and excretion. When a person's intake of fat is high, the levels of cholesterol in the blood can increase. Different types of fat affect the levels of different lipoproteins: LDL cholesterol is a major risk factor in heart disease.

Celery has a phytochemical that—in rats—lowers blood cholesterol levels seven percent and blood pressure by 13 percent. Oriental medicine has long used celery to reduce blood pressure.

Crabmeat contains significant amounts of omega-3 fatty acids.

Balancing cholesterol levels

The effects of dietary fats on cholesterol levels can be very confusing. It may seem reasonable to assume that by reducing the amount of cholesterol in the diet the amount in the blood would also reduce. However this isn't the case; reducing the intake of saturated fat has more of an impact.

High levels of LDL cholesterol are not desirable, but a certain amount of cholesterol is needed to carry out various functions in the cells. Interestingly, we actually manufacture 75 percent of our cholesterol, and the amount is directly related to the quantities of fat eaten.

191

Overall, the portion that comes from the diet has only a small effect on blood levels—that is except for people at risk. Some studies have shown that eating cholesterol increases the risk of heart disease even if it doesn't increase blood cholesterol levels. People with coronary heart disease or risk factors for heart disease and stroke are the most vulnerable.

There are three things we can do to improve the cholesterol situation. Firstly, we can reduce LDL levels by altering the types of fat eaten; less full fat dairy products, fatty meat, and commercially produced cakes and pastries. Secondly, we also need to ensure that HDL levels are not reduced, so we need to eat foods that improve or maintain HDL levels. These include the omega-3 and omega-6 foods listed previously. Thirdly, we need to aim to lower production of LDL, or increase production of HDL and encourage the excretion of LDL. Some foods actively help you to do this. They include a balanced intake of unsaturated fats, the phytochemicals in garlic, soya beans, soymilk, and soluble fiber (oats and pulses). In addition exercise can help lower LDL while moderate amounts of beer and wine may help increase HDL levels.

Finally, there are products on our supermarket shelves—yogurts, margarines, etc. —that actively reduce the overall cholesterol levels and they may help as part of a

If eaten regularly as part of a balanced diet, leeks can help keep cholesterol levels low.

Commercially produced cholesterol reducing products
are a useful addition to many diets.

controlled diet. However these products may also reduce the absorption of antioxidants, which as you've already read about in chapter three are something we want to hang onto.

SUPPLEMENTS

Fish oil

Fish oils supplements are either made from liver oils (obtained from white fish like cod and halibut) or fish oil concentrates (obtained from the flesh of fish like salmon). Cod liver oil is high in EPA, DHA, and also vitamins A and D; fish oil concentrates generally don't include vitamins A and D. If you do decide to take a supplement, when making a choice you must decide what you are taking it for. If it is only to get the RDA of vitamins A and D the most basic one-a-day dose will suffice.

193

However, if you are taking it as protection from cardiovascular disease and rheumatic joints you need to check the label to ensure that EPA and DHA are listed.

Evening primrose oil

As mentioned earlier many women take EPO for the beneficial effects on the menstrual cycle and menopause. Studies have shown that, in conjunction with fish oils, it can be beneficial to arthritis and rheumatism sufferers too. However, to get the desired benefit you need to take a substantial dose: the minimum that would appear to be effective is 2000mg in a single supplement daily and it may take several months before a difference is noticeable. The percentage of GLA (the active ingredient) is not the same in all supplements so do check the label before buying. Many supplements will also include vitamin E to protect against oxidation of polyunsaturated fats (EPO is a PUFA).

Starflower oil (or borage oil) is another source of GLA, containing a higher percentage in total than EPO. It is available as a single supplement or combined with EPO. It has been less researched than EPO, and its chemical structure is different, leading many scientists to think it may not be as effective a source of GLA.

People on anticoagulant drugs should be careful when taking EPO and it is best be avoided by epileptics and schizophrenics. As always check with a doctor before taking more than the RDA of any supplement.

One-a-day cod liver oils capsules can be beneficial to those who need to take large doses to reduce the joint pain of arthritis.

*Chestnuts are the only seriously low fat nuts; when pureed they
have a chocolaty flavor and may be useful to dieters.*

LIPOTROPICS—WHAT ARE THEY?

Lipotropics are fat manipulators; their function is to prevent an abnormal build up of fat in the liver. They have four main functions:

- They increase the production of lecithin by the liver. Lecithin is important as it makes cholesterol soluble, and therefore less likely to be deposited in the gall bladder or blood vessels.
- They prevent build up of fat in the liver.
- They detoxify amines, the products of protein metabolism.
- They increase resistance to disease by helping the thymus gland to carry out its anti-disease functions. (The thymus gland is found near the heart in the chest and its principal function is to secrete hormones that help in antibody production.)

Some people need lipotropics more than others. Those on a high protein diet need a greater intake to detoxify the products of protein metabolism. Most of us eat too much fat; lipotropics are essential to the production of lecithin in the liver to keep cholesterol on the move.

Choline, inostitol, and methionine are all considered to be lipotropics. Betaine is another lipotropic which has been found to significantly reduce homocysteine levels—an amino acid which has been strongly linked with increased cardiovascular disease risk.

Methionine

Methionine is an essential amino acid which, with choline, detoxifies amines, protects the kidneys, and reduces fat in the liver. It also acts as a catalyst for the actions of choline and inositol.

As well as the phtytochemical capsaicin which is an antioxidant, chilies
stimulate metabolic rate and can have a cholesterol lowering effect.

Choline

Choline is found in egg yolks, brain, heart, green leafy vegetables, wheat germ, yeast, liver: the average diet contains 500 and 900mg daily. It is a neurotransmitter in the brain (acetyl choline) but also has a role in emulsifying cholesterol, metabolizing fats, and detoxifying amines. A deficiency of choline is thought to cause cirrhosis and fatty degeneration of the liver, hardening of the arteries, and could have a connection with Alzheimer's disease.

Raisins are a surprising source of inositol as well as potassium and iron.

It has only been recently that the advantages of choline have been properly researched. It is now thought to have a use in the treatment of arteriosclerosis, diabetes, forgetfulness, gall bladder trouble, glaucoma, muscular dystrophy, and senility.

Inositol

Inositol is found in liver, dried lima beans, brewer's yeast, grapefruit, raisins, cantaloupe, wheat germ, cabbage, peanuts. It is destroyed by caffeine. It is known to help in lowering cholesterol levels, and preventing eczema. A deficiency is linked to hair loss. Along with choline it

Cabbage contains high levels of inositol,
known to reduce cholesterol.

has been used in the treatment of nerve and muscular disorders such as multiple sclerosis, muscular dystrophy, and cerebral palsy.

Lecithin

Lecithin is a group of fatty substances, but importantly it is found in large quantities in the human brain. It is present in certain foods (soya beans, egg yolk, trout, whole grains, legumes) and is widely used as a commercial emulsifier, i.e. in margarine and chocolate bars. In the body it helps to maintain the structure of cell membranes as well as keeping fats and cholesterol on the move. There is no proof that it actively lowers blood cholesterol levels, but it is a good source of the neurotransmitter choline. Supplements are sometimes recommended for people suffering dementia-type illnesses.

LOW FAT DIETS: STILL GOOD FOR US?

When it comes to healthy eating many people have misinterpreted the health message that all fat was bad and low fat was good; as a consequence many of us have reduced our fat intake considerably. So much so that we may actually be missing out on essential fatty acids and lipotropics in our diet. If you follow the advice above and include MUFA rich foods in a balanced diet, you may be able to considerably redress the balance to your health advantage.

There are a lot of low fat products on the market today, but you should be aware that low fat does not equal no fat. In many cases it actually means extra sugar and other additives, as manufacturers try to save the flavor. There are many rules that regulate what claims can be made for products labeled low fat, reduced fat, or even fat free: but what you should know is that there is still some fat in all of them.

Such fat replacement products are big business. One of the

Condiments based on oil are high in calories and fat, but the fats present in mayonnaise are mostly MUFA.

goals of food manufacturers is to find a substance that does not detract from taste but also doesn't supply the bad fat. One substance, olestra, was given FDA approval in 1996: beside the possible side effects of abdominal cramping, olestra "inhibits the body's absorption of certain fat-soluble vitamins and nutrients," and vitamins A, D, E, and K have to be added to any foods in which it is used. Commercially it has been used primarily in snack foods and it must carry a health warning about its side effects.

Other products are being developed in order to help with the problem of clinically obese people. The aim is to create a drug that reduces fat absorption. Drug trials are currently being carried out and limited approval has been given for some products.

6. CARBOHYDRATES

As well as oxygen and water, energy is a basic requirement for life. Our body needs a constant supply of energy to carry out its most basic functions: respiration, growth and repair, and to enable movement. Our energy comes from the food and drink we consume. Most foods—except oils and sugar—are a mixture of all the nutrients we need, but ultimately we want the basic unit of energy—glucose—to provide power to run the body's mechanisms.

Glucose is a sugar but is also a carbohydrate. We've heard a lot about carbohydrates over the years. Most of us know them as the bulky fibrous foods that we use to fill up on when we're hungry; they are the foods that can make us sated and sleepy. Did you know sugar—in all its incarnations—is a carbohydrate? Did you know that low fat foods often have a higher sugar content than their counterparts? It's time to start looking at the different types of carbohydrate so we can better understand how they work and what label ingredients really mean.

WHAT ARE CARBOHYDRATES?

Carbohydrates are starches and sugars. They are important for several reasons but primarily they are an energy source and their function is the production and storage of energy within all cells. Chemically they all contain carbon, hydrogen, and oxygen in various ratios. The smallest

Left: Pasta is a staple to the Italian and now many Western diets.

molecules or "units" are glucose and fructose, sugars that are also referred to as monosaccharides. When two types of sugars combine to form more complex molecules they are known as disaccharides (double sugars). Units of glucose and fructose form sucrose; lactose (the sugar found in milk) is units of glucose and galactose. These mono- and disaccharides are all sweet and soluble in water. We also know these sugars as simple carbohydrates.

Under certain conditions, different combinations of monosaccharides link up to form larger, long chain molecules called polysaccharides. These molecules are insoluble, and not sweet. Polysaccharides are excellent storage molecules; when required they can be chemically altered (hydrolyzed) and the smaller monosaccharide

A typical breakfast for many people is a bowl of cereal,
but it has quite a high glycaemic index.

units are released for use as energy. The best known polysaccharides are starch and glycogen: starch is found in plants; glycogen is found in animals and is sometimes called animal starch. Plants store starch, a product of photosynthesis, in their leaves, tubers, and roots; however some plants, such as sugar beets and sugar cane, are able to store sucrose as well. Polysaccharides are also known as complex carbohydrates. Besides their storage potential, polysaccharide carbohydrates are also important to cell structure. Cellulose is used in plants to give strength to their cell walls, and is the main constituent of what we call fiber.

WHERE CAN WE FIND THEM?

Starches are found in large amounts in foods such as flour, grains, pasta, bread, vegetables, and pulses. Sugars occur in large amounts in fruits, some vegetables, and in high quantities in commercially produced foods such as preserves, cakes, and sweet drinks.

We eat both available carbohydrates (sugars and starch) and non-available carbohydrates (cellulose). The non-available carbohydrate is also known as dietary fiber. The available carbohydrates are broken down by digestive enzymes within the body and the constituent monosaccharide units – mainly glucose—are either used as energy immediately or sent to storage. Glucose is converted to glycogen for storage and in animals this is found in the liver, muscles, and fat cells in adipose tissues.

*Potatoes are mostly carbohydrate;
the skins are an excellent source of fiber.*

FIBER

Dietary fiber, found in whole grain breads and cereals, pulses, nuts, and dried fruits, as well as in some fruit and vegetables, is a necessary component of the diet. It helps us to feel full and is also vital for proper functioning of the digestive system, although it provides no energy or nutrients. Insoluble fiber, like cellulose, is important for increasing the bulk of fecal stools, and speeding their passage through the bowel. Dietary fiber helps us to avoid constipation and hemorrhoids and has been shown to be important in the prevention of bowel cancer, diverticulitis, and irritable bowel syndrome (IBS).

Corn is particularly high in fiber, and the kernels are enclosed in indigestible shells.

Some fiber is soluble, such as pectin (found in apples and other fruits), beta-glucans (found in cereals like oats and rye), and arabinose (found in pulses). The soluble fibers are thought to help in the maintenance of blood sugar levels by slowing down sugar absorption, and they may also have a role in reducing LDL cholesterol levels.

In Western countries, we don't have enough fiber in our diets. An average intake of 13g is about half the recommended daily amount (24g). For chronic constipation, a higher intake of 32g with more fluid may help. It is best to get your fiber from whole foods rather than supplements. Most supplements are based on bran which contains compounds (called phytates i.e. phytic acid) that may prevent the absorption of essential micronutrients.

The pectin found in apples is useful for an upset stomach.

Pulses as a group are a highly nutritious food. Although the content of each different pulse varies, they are low in fat, high in protein, high in soluble fiber, and high in complex carbohydrates. Many also contain iron, B vitamins, and trace elements, which makes them especially useful to the diets of non-meat eaters.

Pulses can be toxic however, if not properly prepared; those canned in brine will have a higher sodium content. Soy beans, in particular, have come in for close scrutiny over the years. Soy products have manifold health benefits that derive from their unique constituents: they contain all eight essential amino acids, many phytoestrogens, and small amounts of mostly unsaturated fat. Many people eat soy products to alleviate the symptoms of premenstrual syndrome and the menopause, and they are useful in lowering LDL levels.

Soy products have long been seen as great for vegetarians but we are gradually seeing how beneficial they are to any healthy diet.

EFFECTS OF CARBOHYDRATES ON BODY SYSTEMS

Carbohydrates are metabolized to molecules of readily available energy in the form of glucose (also known as blood sugar) and their metabolism is controlled by insulin. Blood sugar levels rise after a meal; insulin, a hormone secreted by the pancreas, ensures that glucose levels in the blood return to a normal level by stimulating the liver to take up the excess glucose for storage. Diabetes mellitus occurs when this mechanism fails and there is a deficiency of insulin. This means carbohydrate cannot enter most cells for storage.

The action of insulin is balanced by glucagon, another hormone from the pancreas. When blood sugar levels are low (hypoglycemia) insulin decreases and glucagon stimulates the conversion of glycogen to glucose. In addition the "stress" hormones adrenaline and corticosteroid produced by the adrenal glands can act to raise blood sugar levels.

DIABETES

We know of two types of diabetes: diabetes insipidus is a rare disease that has similar symptoms to diabetes mellitus, but is caused by a failure of the pituitary gland to secrete antidiuretic hormone (ADH). It can be present from birth but may occur after kidney disease or taking certain drugs. It can be treated with synthetic ADH or by a low sodium diet and diuretic drugs.

The other form of diabetes is more common. Diabetes mellitus is caused by insufficient or absent insulin production. In its absence blood sugar levels rise and cause the characteristic symptoms of needing to urinate frequently, excessive thirst, and tiredness. With the inability to store glucose, weight loss is also a sign, as is sugar in the urine.

These petit fours look and probably taste delicious, but they are little more than sugar.

Diabetes mellitus occurs in two types. Type I is the more severe form causing insulin dependence and appears between ages 10–16 or under 35. Type II diabetes has a more gradual onset and generally occurs after the age of 40. It can remain hidden for a long time before being diagnosed. Treatment is usually with controlled diet, weight reduction, and oral medication. Type II diabetes mellitus is on the increase in the Western world. We are overloading our bodies with sugar and they just can't cope: obesity is a key factor. Shockingly it is also occurring at much younger ages. Now cases have been seen in teenagers and they are on the rise.

Diabetics are at risk from a variety of ailments, particularly if they do not control their disease and treatment properly. Complications with eyesight and circulation can be forestalled by regular checkups. Diabetics are at higher risk from cardiovascular disorders —atherosclerosis, hypertension—and cataracts.

Gestational diabetes is the term for diabetes that develops when a woman is pregnant, usually in the second half of the pregnancy. The baby may be bigger than expected and the mother produces sugar in her urine. She will not always develop full-blown diabetes, although about 75 percent of cases do.

Many shops sell diabetic foods. You should be careful; some are high in fat and as high in calories as their counterparts. The special foods tend to be high in fructose or sorbitol (a sweetner) and high intakes of both can lead to digestive problems. Instead look for food that is both low in fat and sugar.

ARTIFICIAL SWEETENERS

Over the years several artificial sweeteners have been developed to replace sugars. They are used in many food products and provided as sugar substitutes to put in tea, coffee etc. Saccharin was once widely used, but after concerns about its safety it is now strictly controlled.

Another product, cyclamates were banned by the USA FDA. Aspartame is the most recently developed sweetner. It is actually a naturally occurring amino acid, that is 200 times sweeter than sugar, but some people complain about the aftertaste.

HIGH AND LOW CARBOHYDRATE DIETS

The form in which we eat our carbohydrates is important. Unrefined foods, such as wholemeal bread and pasta, brown rice, pulses, fresh fruit, and vegetables have not been processed in any way and contain all their original nutrients. Refined carbohydrates are foods that have been processed in some way: either they have lost their fiber content or they

Pastries and pies can be made less dangerous to your carbohydrate intake by using sugar substitutes.

have been added to another product during manufacture. A high intake of refined carbohydrates, such as sugar, white flour, white pasta, and white rice can lead to obesity and dental decay. Obesity in turn can contribute to diabetes and arthritis and result in other health dilemnas.

Low carbohydrate diets tend to lead to eating a greater proportion of fat and protein. A greater proportion of the protein in a low-carbohydrate diet will come from meat and cheese, and therefore be higher in saturated fats. An increase in the wrong type of fat in the diet is linked with an increased risk of heart disease, some cancers, especially bowel cancer, constipation, and obesity. High carbohydrate diets depend on the type of carbohydrate; if you eat a lot of sugar it is not so good! A diet that contains a large

Wild and unrefined rice has the lower glycaemic index. The less sticky a rice is the better it is for you—basmati has a very low GI.

amount of unrefined foods, in particular vegetables and pulses, is probably better for you, not only because it's packed with micronutrients.

Most health departments and dieticians recommend that the bulk of our daily food intake should be carbohydrate. The figures vary a bit though: in the USA the amount suggested is 55 percent, while WHO recommend 55 to 75 percent. At the moment about 60 percent of the carbohydrates we eat are starches and 40 percent sugars. Ideally a balanced diet is not just about eating high or low quantities of carbohydrates: it's down to eating the right sort. The bulk of our intake should be complex carbohydrates and what are classified as intrinsic sugars. Intrinsic sugars are those found in fruit and vegetables which are bound up in the cellular structure of the food. Extrinsic sugars are found in fruit drinks, honey, cookies, cakes etc.—i.e. a lot of commercially produced items—and are a major contributor toward tooth decay.

GLYCAEMIC INDEX

The carbohydrates that are best for us are those which are unrefined and with a low glycaemic index. The glycaemic index (GI) was developed to help in the treatment of diabetes. It measures the rate at which blood glucose levels rise after a particular carbohydrate food is eaten. Glucose has a rating of 100 (the highest) because it is readily absorbed; the lower the GI rating the slower the food is absorbed. Foods with low GI rating will help you to feel full for longer and are useful in slimming diets to keep blood sugar levels stable.

The GI rating of this doughnut will be very high!

Although fat and protein aren't measured using the index they do have an impact on the GI of other foods. Generally, they lower a food's GI rating, so it's a good idea for every meal or snack to consist of a bit of all three macronutrients. The slow digestion and more stable blood sugar level have several benefits for many people. Low GI foods:

- Work to keep insulin levels lower, making it easier to burn fat, and so less likely that it is stored.
- Actively keep blood fats (lipoproteins) at lower levels.
- Tend to reduce hunger and appetites as they are more satisfying.
- Can help to reduce the risk of developing diabetes and heart disease.

There are other factors that influence the GI of various foods. Some cooking methods increase the amount of gelatinized starch, such as in cornflakes, and this increases the GI. In addition, by removing the outer fibrous layer of some vegetables and grains we are removing a barrier of fiber that would slow down digestion of the food. The constituents of the food also have a bearing on the GI. Starch can be divided into two types: amylose or amylopection; the more amylopectin in a food the higher the GI. As you might expect, the greater the soluble fiber in a food, the lower its GI.

You should note that there are no GI values for meat, nuts, and avocados because they contain little or no carbohydrates. The figures in the brackets in the following list indicate the GI values.

Cherries have a low GI value contributing to lower lipid levels.

214

Low GI foods:

Pulses: butter beans (31), chickpeas (33), kidney beans (boiled 27, canned and drained 52), lentils (30), soya beans (18).

Fruit: apples (38), cherries (22), dried apricots (31), grapefruit (25), peaches (42), plums (39).

Vegetables: broccoli, Brussels sprouts, green beans, leafy greens, leeks, mange-tout, mushrooms, onions, peppers, spinach, zucchini (courgettes): all very low.

Other: Natural yogurt (14), milk (full fat 27; skimmed 32), peanuts (14), barley (25).

Not all fruit has a low GI but these dried apricots do.

Mid range GI foods:

Wheat: All bran (42), noodles (40), oat bran (55), oatmeal biscuits (54), porridge (42), white or whole wheat pasta (45), buckwheat (54), bulgar (48), pitta bread (57), rice (basmati 58, instant 86), whole grain rye bread (86).

Fruit and veg: Cantaloupe (65), grapes (46), kiwi fruit (52), mangoes (55), oranges (55), peas (48), sweet potatoes (54), boiled potatoes (62), sweet corn (55), yams (51).

High GI foods:

Fruit and veg: baked or mashed potatoes (85), bananas (55), cooked carrots (49), parsnips (87), pineapple (66), raisins (64), squash, swede (72), watermelon (72).

Wheat: Bagel (72), French baguette (95) wholemeal bread (69), white

bread (70), rice cakes (82), couscous (65), breadsticks, Gluten free bread (90).

Cereals: cornflakes (84), bran flakes, puffed cereals (80), popcorn, muffins (apple 44, blueberry 59).

Other: Taco shells (68), French fries (75), jelly beans, potato chips (54).

The GI index is measured per 100g and the value for some foods may confuse you. Most vegetables have a low GI, in particular salad, and you can eat moderate amounts with causing too much of a blood sugar surge. In addition, as a guideline, dense breads such as pumpernickel, sourdough, or those made with stone ground flour also have a lower GI than other types. In essence low GI eating means putting the emphasis on whole grains and legumes—barley, oats, rye, peas, and

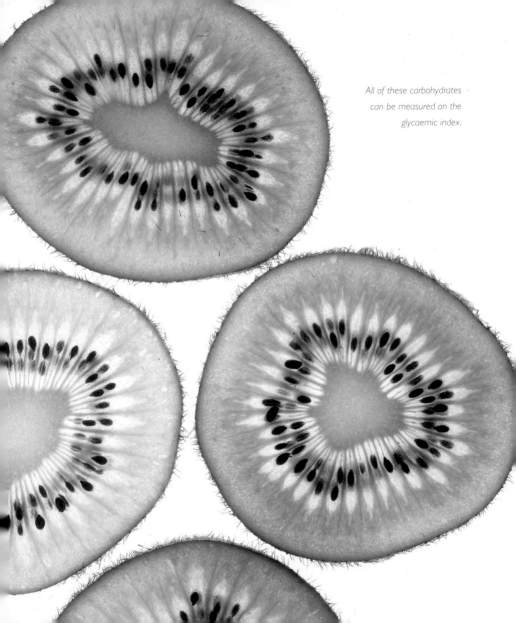

All of these carbohydrates
can be measured on the
glycaemic index.

The best granola, with the lowest GI, will have lots of whole grains.

beans—in combination with certain types of bread, pasta, and rice, as well as vegetables and fruit.

Celiac disease

Celiac disease is an uncommon condition in which the small intestine is damaged by gluten, a protein found in wheat, barley, and rye. Symptoms in adults include vague tiredness, weight loss, and swelling of the legs. Celiac disease tends to run in families. Treatment, if lifelong, is avoidance of foods and products of wheat, rye, barley, and many sufferers are told to avoid oats as well. Many specially manufactured gluten-free products are available but there is no restriction on dairy products, vegetables, fruit, rice, or corn.

GI – WHY IT MIGHT KEEP YOU HEALTHY

A lot of research is being carried out looking at the effect of GI foods on lifestyle and overall health, particularly with regard to diabetes. One study followed a group of women over a period of 10 years; those who had diets with high GI content were at twice the risk of having a heart attack than those on low GI diets. It's looking like it comes down to the blood lipoproteins: low GI food has a role to play in keeping them stable—and may also help with blood clotting factors. Studies on young people with obesity problems has led to the conclusion that high GI foods can promote a series of hormonal and metabolic events that actually encourages excess food intake in obese subjects. With regard to sport, studies are still ongoing to see if high GI foods are useful during and after exercise, but it looks like low GI foods are helpful in endurance sports, such as cycling.

You may find it interesting to note that the highly recommended Mediterranean style diet, although quite high in carbohydrates

Noodles from Asia, brought to Italy by Marco Polo, have long been thought to be the precursor to spaghetti.

—think of all that pasta—actually incorporates low GI carbohydrates. In addition it is high in the right kind of fats (MUFA) that promotes low levels of LDL and high levels of HDL cholesterol. In one study, the participants' HDL levels were measured and the type of foods eaten noted. It was shown that HDL levels correlated with the glycaemic index of the diet—the higher the GI, the lower the levels of HDL. Asian style diets are advantageous for the same reasons. Studies have shown that the Mediterranean and Asian style diets are probably responsible for the low incidence of cancer and cardiovascular disease in these parts of the world.

Sushi is an excellent low fat, high MUFA,
high protein meal, but the rice here is high GI.

Now we know what is required for a healthy diet, we should perhaps consider the forms that any food supplements take. Ideally we want to achieve a fully balanced diet through eating the right foods. When this is not possible—through ill health, pregnancy, or at certain times when our bodies are undergoing biological changes (for example, the menopause)—taking single or multivitamin and mineral supplements can make a real difference.

The first thing to decide is what supplements may be beneficial to your diet and lifestyle. This book will hopefully help. However, if you are at all worried, you should check with your health practitioner for more specific diagnosis and advice.

Next you need to understand the basics about the choices available in the pots and bottles on the pharmacist's shelves: what are the important ingredients and values to look for?

Why do you want a nutritional supplement?

Do you want a high or low strength dose? If you are taking a supplement as a form of nutritional insurance, to prevent a deficiency, or to maintain health, then lower potency, multiingredient products will work in these instances.

If you want to combat a deficiency, meet a specific nutritional requirement, or improve certain aspects of your health then a higher potency, individual product would probably be better.

Left: Vitamin C is the most popular supplement, but you'd get much more from this kiwi.

Range of nutrients

A general product labeled as being a multivitamin and mineral supplement may not always mean you get a comprehensive range of nutrients —it could contain only 10 or so—and it may not contain the right mix for you.

Ingredients

It is important to check the list of ingredients, especially if you have any allergies or other dietary restrictions. Watch out if you require products that are yeast-free, suitable for vegan and vegetarian diets, or gluten-free. Beware of labels that declare "no added sugar" but have plenty of artificial sweeteners.

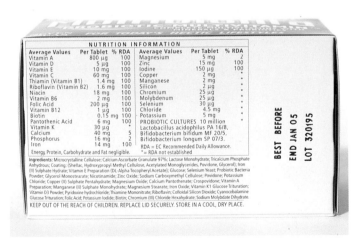

You can learn a lot by looking at labels. Make sure that you are getting the best form of each ingredient, and look at the amount each supplement delivers.

Prices

The most expensive supplements are not always the best: they are sometimes just the most expensive. However, if you are on a budget, price could influence the supplement that you buy. In this case it is even more important that you read the label to ensure you are getting what you require. If you cannot understand the label, ask the pharmacist to clarify. If he or she can't, go elsewhere to another pharmacist that can!

FORM: PILL, POTION, OR POWDER

Nutritional supplements come in various forms: tablets, liquids, capsules, powders etc., and, depending on your circumstances, some may be better for you than others.

Pills, liquid, or powder; you may need to try different types to find the best source for you.

If your kids are developing normally and are active, they probably don't need a vitamin supplement.

• **Chewable tablets** are seen more now and are primarily aimed at delivering supplements for children. The main advantage is they can be taken without water. They are frequently flavored and some may contain sugar or sweeteners.

• **Tablets (effervescent)** have been around for many years and are a popular way to take vitamin C. While not an unpleasant way to take a supplement, it can be expensive and contain additives or flavorings.

• **Hard gelatin capsules** are usually of animal origin. Gelatin is derived from animal, usually bovine, collagen. There are some capsules that are starch or seaweed-based, but they are not as

Cod liver oil in liquid form is not to everyone's taste.

widely available. The capsules provide a unit dose of a powder or occasionally liquid supplement and are readily broken down in the gut. They contain fewer nonactive (excipient) ingredients and many people think they are easier to swallow than tablets; they may be pulled apart and the ingredients taken separately.

• **Liquids** are the traditional presentation of some supplements, for instance cod liver oil or royal jelly. Liquids are easily absorbed and are particularly advantageous for those who find taking tablets difficult. While they may also be a good way to take a higher potency supplement, it may be difficult to control the dose unless a proper measuring device is used. Many liquid supplements contain high levels of sugar or sweeteners to disguise the taste.

• **Powders** are used only occasionally for supplement delivery, and usually require mixing with liquid before being taken. They are not very portable and there is a possible risk of contamination.

• **Soft gelatin capsules** are used mainly for liquid supplements and are made from a mixture of glycerin and animal gelatin. Research has shown that these capsules are easiest to swallow.

• **Tablets** are the most frequently seen form for nutrient supplements. They are made by mixing together the relevant ingredients in powder form and applying high pressure. They contain several ingredients that

have no nutritional effect and act as stabilizers for the vitamins and minerals. Unlike the gelatin capsule tablets, they are more suitable for vegetarians and vegans and are less expensive.

• **Slow release preparations** are a more sophisticated way of taking supplements. Due to the efficient way the body excretes surplus vitamins (particularly the water-soluble ones) and minerals it can be hard to maintain a constant supply. Many nutritionists recommend slow release preparations with staggered delivery so as not to saturate the body with excess supplements, and to prevent wastage.

Liquid supplements are sometimes easier to take in capsule form, as the taste moment is a lot shorter and doesn't linger.

Slow release preparations have special coatings that are designed to gradually release nutrients over a six- to eight-hour period. The tablet core is slowly eroded as it passes through the digestive tract. They should always be taken with or just after food.

WHAT ELSE IS IN A SUPPLEMENT?

Depending on the presentation of a supplement it may contain several other non-active ingredients. These "excipients" can be necessary to help bind the supplement formulation together and improve product processing.

Binders give materials more cohesion, enabling the ingredients to stick together. Cellulose and ethyl cellulose are the most frequently seen, though gum arabic (acacia), algin (sodium alginate or alginic acid), lecithin, and sorbitol are also used.

Coatings. A variety of substances are used to prevent the supplement from being damaged by moisture. They can also hide nasty flavors, smells, and make tablets easier to swallow. Carnuba wax, shellac, and beeswax are used as glazing agents in tablet coatings.

Colors are usually added for aesthetic reasons. The colors used are derived from chemical—titanium dioxide (white) and iron oxide (red)—and natural sources: annatto, curcumin, chlorophyll, and anthocyanins. Riboflavin (vitamin B2) is a naturally occurring yellow dye.

Disintegrators are substances that enable the easy collapse of the tablet after digestion such as maize starch, modified starch, and croscarmellose sodium (carboxymethylcellulose).

Drying agents prevent materials from absorbing moisture during processing; silica gel is the most common.

Fillers or **dilutents** are usually inert (non-reactive) and are used to increase bulk. Dicalcium phosphate is a white powder used as a source of calcium and phosphorus and as a bulking and binding agent. Sorbitol and cellulose are also used. Copovidone is a bulking agent.

Flavors and **sweeteners.** Various flavors used are citrus oils, vanilla, and cocoa. Sweeteners can be sugars: sucrose, glucose (dextrose), lactose, fructose, maltose, raw cane sugar, glucose syrup, corn syrup, honey; sugar alcohols: maltodextrin, sorbitol, mannitol, and xylitol; artificial sweeteners: saccharin, aspartame, and acesulphame K.

Lubricants are used to prevent tablets from sticking to machinery. Magnesium stearate and stearic acid are fat-based lubricants that stop tablets sticking together during compression.

You may also see any of the following on a label:

- Lactose, sorbitol, xylitol: bulking agents and used to aid compression, as well as having a sweetening effect.
- Methyl cellulose (hydroxypropyl methyl cellulose, hydroxypropyl cellulose): used as glazing agents they give a smooth coating to tablets. Of natural origin they are also used as slow release agents.
- Microcrystalline cellulose: a binding and disintegrating agent.
- Polysorbate 80 (E433): an emulsifier.
- Silicon dioxide (silica), magnesium silicate, talc: these ingredients help powders to move more smoothly through machinery.
- Vegetable fat (hydrogenated vegetable fat): used as a lubricant and slow release agent in levels that are not significant to daily diet.

UNITS

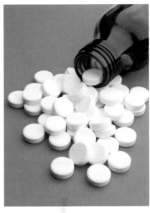

After deciphering the ingredients and contents of the nutritional supplement, it is also important to have an understanding of the quantity of each component in the supplement. National bodies have produced recommended daily allowances (RDA) or reference nutrient intake (RNI) as suggested by European agencies. Some practitioners feel that these allowances are not adequate, and it should be noted that they are recommendations only. It is difficult to overdose on water-soluble vitamins, but you should be careful taking megadoses of fat-soluble vitamins. Pregnant women should not take vitamin A except on the recommendation of their health practition-

A common form in which many pills are produced. Did we ever realize how much goes into it?

er or antenatal clinic. Minerals are required in only trace amounts for specific functions and taking doses over the RDA could be toxic.

Labels will frequently list the following units:

- IU or iu – international units
- mg – milligrams; 1mg = 0.001g (one thousandth of a gram)
- mcg/µg – micrograms; 1µg = 0.001mg (one thousandth of a milligram)
- RE – retinol equivalents. Used specifically for vitamin A; it measures the amount of vitamin A actually absorbed and converted.

In addition many labels also state what percentage of the daily RDA is delivered by the supplement.

WHAT TO LOOK FOR

Many vitamins are made directly from natural products, but in the vast majority of cases the products are synthesized chemically. The vitamins synthesized by a manufacturer are mostly identical to those found in nature, but not always. Occasionally synthetic vitamins taken in high doses can cause toxic reactions. Intake of high doses of naturally-obtained vitamins do not seem to cause the same problems. In addition they are combined with constituents that are also useful: vitamin A from rosehips also contains bioflavonoids which can help the action of vitamin C. Naturally occurring vitamin E is a complex of tocopherols, including one, d-alpha tocopherol, which when synthesized is dl-alpha tocopherol. Synthesized vitamin E is not as active, weight for weight, as that derived from a natural source.

Minerals are inorganic substances that occur in nature and cannot be manufactured. Many supplements use inorganic minerals salts (compounds) of the minerals. Plants absorb minerals from the soil: animals obtain their minerals from eating plants or other animals that have eaten plants. Some practitioners believe that organic chelated minerals—minerals available in a particular type of compound—are more effectively assimilated should be used in preference to non-chelated versions.

STORAGE

It is important to follow the storage instructions for supplements, in order that they retain their potency. Keep them in their original packaging and away from direct sunlight.

Developing children often suffer growing pains and extra calcium, magnesium, and phosphorus is recommended, either by diet or supplement.

An apple a day…

This final chapter is going to look at the changes our bodies go through in life, from childhood to old age and look at specific nutritional requirements we might have at different times of life.

DON'T LOSE THOSE NUTRIENTS

Whatever your stage of life there are some ways to make sure that you make the most of the nutritional potential of the food you eat. Many vitamins are destroyed by food processing, overlong storage, and cooking methods. The following list is just some guidelines that may prove beneficial.

- Most fruit and vegetables should be kept in the fridge until needed. If they are stored in light and at warmer temperatures they tend to lose vitamin C more rapidly than in cooler conditions. (There are exceptions: bananas should be kept in cool place, potatoes should be kept in the cool and dark but not a fridge.)
- Wash vegetables before using them but don't soak as you'll lose B complex and vitamin C.
- Avoid chopping or peeling fruit and vegetables until the last minute: fruit and vegetables cut up and left to stand lose vitamins and begin to oxidize.
- Potatoes store a lot of nutrients in their skins, so by removing them you lose out; bake or boil them in their skins for maximum potential.

- Water used in the cooking of vegetables can be used as the basis for stocks and soups.
- Don't thaw frozen vegetables before cooking.
- If you aren't going to eat fruit and vegetables within three days or so, it's worth not buying so much or buying frozen. Many frozen vegetables contain higher levels of vitamin C because of the speed at which they are processed.
- Defrost all meat and fish products completely before cooking, unless the product's instructions advise otherwise. (If you defrost items in the microwave, turn them from time to time to ensure that the process is even).
- To retain the maximum amount of nutrients in your vegetables, cook them in the least volume of water for the shortest time.
- Light can be destructive: bread can loose valuable nutrients if exposed, and milk stored in glass loses vitamins B2 (riboflavin), A, and D unless kept out of the light.

BOOSTING YOUR NUTRIENTS

There are specific times in everyone's life when extra nutrients are required. The early years of life proceed at a rapid pace of growth and development, while at the other end of the scale, older age frequently brings with it various ailments and a reduced appetite. Keen sports people, whether amateur or professional will also have specific nutritional needs for peak performance. All stages of life can generally be enhanced by minor changes to diet or lifestyle for a positive benefit.

CHILDHOOD

The early years in every child's life are marked by distinctive development milestones. The move from an all liquid diet to adding a bit of solid food; learning to sit up, crawl, and then walk; learning to talk, play, and run. For each stage nutrition is a key parameter that can actively help energy and behavior levels.

From birth to four months, babies need very little else than breast milk, although many are given a vitamin K injection at birth. Breast milk is extremely nutritious, containing compounds that can reduce gastroenteritis, and protect against asthma, eczema, and jaundice. It's thought that breast milks sets you up for life by also offering protection against food allergies and conferring longer-term

A lot of milk comes in see-through glass or plastic bottles, which is alright for the vitamin content because most fridges are dark until the door opens.

immunity. It delivers the essential fatty acids which may help brain development—it appears that breast fed children have higher IQs than bottle-fed children. There are many well known advantages to breast milk—it's free, convenient, and easily digested—but there are many people who have survived being bottle fed too! Formula milk for babies provides adequate nutrition, although some may not receive sufficient selenium.

237

*As well as nutritional benefits, breast feeding is a
time when mother and baby bond closely.*

When children are weaned at around the age of four months, breast milk may not be supplying adequate amounts of some minerals such as copper, iron, zinc, and vitamins A and D, as well as protein. Through the stages of weaning, new tastes and textures are introduced. Sweet drinks should never be given in a bottle and not at nap or bedtime; salt should never be added to food for children being weaned, although you should aim to get them used to a food that resem-

Milk is still useful to deliver a range of nutrients to growing toddlers, but cow's milk should not be used as a main drink until children are a year old.

Weaning can be a messy business, but try to give a variety of tastes and textures.

bles the meals that the rest of the family eat.

In the preschool years, children have a greater need for fat and, aside from breast milk, a good source is full fat milk, as well as yogurts and cheese. Also they don't need as much fiber (proportionally) as older children or adults. It's now taken as a fairly obvious general precaution not to give nuts to small children; not only can they easily choke on them, but there is a growing number who are allergic, especially to peanuts.

239

If a child is growing well on the diet it receives, is active and healthy, then it is probably getting all the nutrients in adequate quantities. You can check your child's progress against height and weight charts that most doctors have. However, if a child seems to be declining you should consult a physician. In a small percentage of preschool children, there may be a need for greater vitamin A, iron, and zinc.

Chewable vitamins are readily available nowadays and most don't have artificial colors, flavors, or sugar, but check the label. Sugar or sweeteners used to be added to make the taste more pleasant to the junior palate. Large sugar intake in children is linked to hyperactivity—have you heard of or seen a sugar rush? It is therefore recommend that you avoid giving young children too many sugary snacks and drinks. Commercially produced products can also contain too much saturated fat and should be limited in a varied diet.

Active and social children are generally healthy kids.

240

TEENAGE

Growing children need to ensure they get their daily intake of calcium and iron to promote normal growth. They should also ensure adequate intake of B complex including folic acid and vitamin C. In school age children there may often be a "battle" of good versus junk food, and possible faddy eating. It's a battle that can be won as children's tastes evolve as they grow, and by not forcing the issue you may succeed in improving their diet.

The ages 13–18 are particularly important for children. It's at this time that they increase muscle and body mass while also developing sexually. It's important that girls get adequate iron during the teenage years, but boys shouldn't miss out either: iron levels have been linked to academic performance. Calcium and folic acid are important for growth and development at this time too.

Teenagers frequently have changeable eating habits, but in particular the uptake of vegetarian or vegan diets is popular. At this time, protein, iron, and folate levels should be carefully watched and supplemented if inadequate. If you are worried about a teenager's eating habits, ensure they take a daily multivitamin and mineral preparation as a form of health insurance.

Watching over what they eat is difficult once they've left home. Students are notorious for having a very unhealthy lifestyle: late nights, not enough rest, poor food intake, too much alcohol etc. A supplement regime including B complex, vitamin E, and choline may help. However, taking supplements is not a substitute for a healthy diet.

YOUNG ADULTS

Young adults between the ages of 20 and 35 are often not very worried about their health and fitness levels. However, it should be noted that bone mass is still being built up at this time: it's essential to get enough

Young adults spend a lot of time "living now" without thinking of later consequences. How you act in your 20s and 30s can affect your health later.

calcium, and to do weight bearing exercise to minimize the potential effects of osteoporosis later in life. Eating pulses, tofu, leafy green vegetables, nuts, and seeds will convey beneficial effects.

In early adulthood, metabolic rate remains fairly constant, until the age of about 30, after which it begins to slow down and weight control becomes a bigger issue. Weight is a factor in several ailments; keeping it at a reasonable level can be a way of preventing arthritis, coronary heart disease, diabetes, and in women, breast cancer. It is important to ensure you get enough phytochemicals and antioxidants for their added protection against the major diseases.

Brain power can be adversely effected by diet during these years, and big meals or crash dieting can be deleterious. Watch the saturated fat intakes, you want to promote the right sort of cholesterol in the blood to improve circulation through the brain. Protein breakfasts and low carbohydrate lunches may improve concentration and memory. A good night's sleep is more important in the 30s and 40s for regeneration and repair to body systems.

Those working in stressful environments, salespeople, hospital workers, and long distance drivers, should increase their B complex to help with the stress but they should also keep vitamin C

Stress and pressure to succeed at work can cause sleeplessness; search out tryptophan and vitamin D.

levels high to ward off infection. Night workers are at risk of missing out on vitamin D. Adjusting to shifts can wreak havoc with your circadian (day/night) rhythms, it's helpful to increase the tryptophan intake in order to sleep better—turkey and lettuce are good sources.

FERTILITY AND CONCEPTION

Following a healthy diet is the first positive step when it comes to preparing for conception. If a mother is healthy before conception and during pregnancy, it can have a beneficial impact on both her recovery after the birth, and also on the health of the baby.

Healthwise, obesity and low weight can both affect female fertility. A certain proportion of body fat is required to help regulate hormone levels; too little or too much can be detrimental. Women who over exercise or have highly restrictive diets may have difficulty conceiving. Slowing down and altering eating habits can be beneficial.

Men trying to boost their fertility should consider vitamins E and C, zinc, and selenium levels. Giving up smoking and reducing caffeine intake will impact positively on fertility levels, as will eating organically: chemical residues may reduce fertility.

*Happy families can take time to create if you
are missing vital micronutrients from your diet.*

PREGNANCY AND BREAST FEEDING

Pregnant women have particular and precise nutritional requirements. Luckily we also know pretty much what they are. It is one time when many people take a supplement and they should be high potency. There is an increased requirement for folic acid in the diet (to avoid neural tube defects as mentioned earlier), and vitamins A, B6, B12, and multiple minerals are needed to promote growth and development. Calcium is especially required in teenage pregnancies. High levels of vitamin A are toxic during pregnancy and can cause birth defects; most women will get enough from their diet.

Extra vitamin C is needed in the last three months and vitamin D should preferably come from a diet high in eggs and oily fish, and full fat diary products. Essential fatty acids, particularly DHA may be especially important in the last months of pregnancy for fetal brain development.

244

Despite the myth, eating for two is not necessary and an extra 200 calories a day will suffice. In general, the metabolic rate slows down and pregnant women do become less active. Many women suffer from constipation, so adding more fiber and water to the diet could help ease the problem.

Nursing mothers need the same micronutrients as pregnant women, and should exercise the same precautions.

Many hormone changes take place when you are pregnant, but take care with supplements.

MIDDLE YEARS

Between the ages of 45 and 65 many changes happen. Women will go through the menopause which has a tremendous impact on body chemistry, and it's now believed that men can go through a similar change.

Symptoms of the menopause in men can be seen in a reduced sex drive, depression or moodiness, weight gain or loss, loss of hair or skin tone. Many of the problems can be resolved or improved by a healthier diet that takes into account a slowing metabolism, and a bit of activity. At this time of life some men may also suffer from problems of an enlarged prostate. This can occur as a result of chemical changes in testosterone in the prostate which changes into a similar but different chemical which causes increased growth of cells, leading to overall enlargement. A diet high in zinc and vitamin E can help alleviate the symptoms.

245

Osteoporosis is a serious condition that mainly affects women after the menopause, but can affect both men and women of a younger age too.

Often called brittle bone disease, osteoporosis occurs when skeletal bone loses density and becomes thinner and more fragile, which is a natural part of aging. After the age of 35 our bone tissue begins to lose more calcium than it can replace. Estrogen is known to have a protective effect against bone thinning but after the menopause estrogen levels drop dramatically.

The best method to deal with osteoporosis is prevention, ensuring adequate diet rich in calcium, magnesium, and phosphorus as well as vitamin D and essential fatty acids. Other micronutrients that should be beneficial to bone health include vitamins C, K, B6, and folic acid, zinc, and potassium. Peak bone mass can be negatively affected by excess alcohol intake, a sedentary lifestyle (weight bearing exercise like walking will make a substantial difference), high salt intake (increase calcium excretion), and inadequate intake of the essential nutrients required for optimum bone health.

At the time of the menopause, women can benefit from soy products which are rich in phytoestrogens which mimic natural estrogens, or they can take hormone replacement therapy (HRT). HRT is not suitable for everyone, but it has a marked effect on preventing bone loss at the menopause.

LATER YEARS

Senior citizens have a widely varying nutrition status: it depends on how active or incapacitated they may be, as well as any ailments of old age that contribute to their lifestyle. Older people require fewer calories, mostly because they become less active and body mass decreases. Although the metabolism is still slower, the need for micronutrients does not reduce. Intake of the minerals calcium, magnesium, and iron, and vitamins B complex, C, D, and E are still essential, although with older age comes a reduced ability to absorb some nutrients. The use of prescription

The effects of old age can be limited by staying active and eating a range of essential foods.

drugs to control some disorders in later years can also affect micronutrient absorption.

Foods need to be selected carefully to achieve the best balance, and in addition fiber is incredibly important. Many older people have a tendency to eat less fresh fruit and vegetables and a higher proportion of commercially produced food, including cakes and cookies; the avoidance of excess sweet food should be seen as a wise precaution as there is a high incidence of sugar diabetes in older people.

Some diseases are more prevalent in the over 65 age group: cancer, coronary heart disease, and stroke. Following a diet early on in life and sticking with it could help prevent or minimize the effects of these disorders. A diet high in antioxidants, fresh fruit and vegetables,

Many people are pleased by the research that show red wine is actually good for us in moderate quantities.

Both red wine and veined cheeses are known to be triggers that exacerbate arthritis.

oily fish, and low in animal fats and overall calories will prove to be worthwhile.

The immune system becomes weaker in later years and it can be boosted by ensuring adequate intake of zinc. In post-menopausal women smoking is a risk factor in bone density loss, as is lack of exercise.

Arthritis

There are two types of arthritis: osteoarthritis and rheumatoid arthritis. Osteoarthritis management does not appear to be affected by diet whereas rheumatoid arthritis can be aided or aggravated by it.

Rheumatoid arthritis is an inflammatory condition that affects the joints, and it is common in adult women. Some foods such as red wine, veined cheese, and anchovies exacerbate symptoms in many people. Elimination diets may help pinpoint the rogue foods causing symptoms to intensify. Diets including high intakes of antioxidants such as vitamins C and E with vitamin D, essential fatty acids such as omega-3 oils and GLA can be extremely beneficial, reducing pain and improving mobility.

Higher levels of vitamin A, C, and E apparently slow progression of the disease. Low selenium can also be a factor, so boost them by eating more nuts, pulses, and oily fish.

Garlic is so good for you, how can you not add it to your diet?

Memory loss

Poor memory can affect most of us at sometime. Haven't we all found ourselves in the position of saying "what was I doing?" or "what did I come here for?" In order to keep the memory functioning properly, a good intake of antioxidants, including vitamin E and B group vitamins, thiamine (B1) in particular, is essential. Many women report a dip in memory power during the menopause, while some younger women find memory affected for a few days before a period is due.

Ginkgo bilboa and Siberian ginseng are both claimed to increase brain capacity, while excessive alcohol intake will have the reverse effect.

In later life forgetfulness can be an early indicator of a more serious dementia. Alzheimer's disease can occur in people around the age of 50 or earlier, and is typified by poor short-term memory, severe memory loss, and confusion. There are theories, as yet unproven, that zinc, selenium, and coenzyme 10 are helpful in preventing the onset, but we do know that vitamin E can slow the disease's progress.

Heart conditions

Coronary heart disease is a big killer, with several well- known risk factors that include smoking, heavy drinking, stress, lack of exercise, high blood cholesterol, and high blood pressure. Easy measures to prevent or reduce the impact of the risk factors are fairly obvious; lose excess weight, reduce alcohol consumption, give up smoking, reduce stress. A diet low in saturated fats but high in garlic, fish oils, soy products, and antioxidants will be beneficial.

One factor that has been linked to strokes is a hormone called homocysteine, which is found in the blood. It appears that low levels of B vitamins and folic acid correlate with higher levels of homocysteine. B vitamins can be obtained from leafy green vegetables and pulses.

Cancer

An anticancer diet should include a high intake of a wide variety of fruit and vegetables to garner their antioxidant protection. In particular tomatoes, broccoli, watercress, Brussels sprouts, carrots, yams, and citrus fruits. Adequate fiber intake is important to keep the bowl healthy; low fiber levels are linked to bowel, breast, and prostate cancer. Diets high in saturated fat have long been linked with cancer, and some good advice is to reduce overall fat intake, but ensure that you don't miss out on the monounsaturated fats that are so essential to well being.

It's the range and quantity of phytochemicals in broccoli that give it such huge anticancer potential.

Sports Nutrition

Sports nutrition is a precise and well-researched science nowadays. There are specialists who can give prescribe a personal diet plan to help you perform better at your chosen sport. Even if you are eating a very healthy diet, if you are exercising frequently or training for a big event there are nutrients you should make sure you don't miss out on, and some you should actively try to get more of. Athletes have very demanding needs for energy, in particular for high-energy food. A diet of increased carbohydrates and proteins is good for those doing action sports. Excess amounts of sugar can have a dehydrating effect and can add to problems in endurance performances. Athletes need to make sure they are getting enough of the key micronutrients, including vitamins B complex, C, and E.

Runners and joggers burn up a lot of glucose during the first 15 to 20 minutes of their exercising, then they start to utilize fats: polyunsaturated fats burn quicker than animal fats. For optimum performance, a diet rich in seeds and nuts will supply some of the necessary substances to avoid free radical build up and should include a bundle of antioxidants vitamins A, C, E, and selenium.

Anyone who is putting pressure on their body to perform should also keep their calcium, magnesium, and phosphorus levels boosted. In addition, vitamin E can help to ward off muscle soreness after the exercise.

Right: Active sports require active control of your diet; the older you get the more difficult it is to take part without including adequate micronutrients to your diet.

Acknowledgments

The publisher would like to thank Digitial Vision for supplying all of the images, including the cover and back photography, in this book. Other photography was supplied as follows;

Pages 2, 28, 36, 39, 48, 104 (bottom), 109, 121, 133, 181, 184, 187, 191, 193, 194, 200, 201, 198, 224, 227, courtesy of Simon Clay;

Pages 5, 11, 15, 69, 95 (bottom), 100, 124, 125 (bottom), 130, 216 (bottom), 217, 134, 141, courtesy of Collins and Brown, part of Chrysalis Books.

Page 92 courtesy of " Ralf A. Clevenger/CORBIS;

Page 245 courtesy of " Laura Doss/Corbis;

Page 247 courtesy of " R.W. Jones/Corbis;

Pages 7, 14, 17, 20, 21, 25, 32, 33, 42, 44, 49, 54, 62, 65, 66, 71, 76, 85, 87, 88 (top), 89, 93, 95 (top), 97, 99, 104 (top), 106, 111, 112, 113, 125 (top), 150, 151-152, 167, 172, 177, 183, 186, 189, 195, 216 (bottom), courtesy of Chrysalis Images.